rockschool®

Guitar
US Level 5 (UK Grade 5)

Performance pieces, technical exercises and in-depth guidance for Rockschool assessments

All accompanying and supporting audio can be downloaded from: *www.rslawards.com/downloads*

Input the following code when prompted: **JMDW23X7G6**

For more information, turn to page 4

www.rslawards.com

Acknowledgements

Published by Rockschool Ltd. © 2012, 2018 & 2020
Catalogue Number: RSK200047US
ISBN: 978-1-78936-143-8
Initial US Release | Errata details can be found at www.rslawards.com/errata

CONTACTING ROCKSCHOOL
www.rslawards.com
Telephone: +44 (0)345 460 4747
Email: info@rslawards.com

Syllabus Director
Tim Bennett-Hart

Head of Graded Music & Publishing
Jono Harrison

2018 Syllabus Repertoire
Produced by Nik Preston

Proof reading
Sharon Kelly, Calum Harrison, Jono Harrison, Nik Preston
(and all arrangers/performers)

US Book Editions (2020)
Additional design work by Steven Price (51 Degrees Design)
and Simon Troup (Digital Music Art)
Edited by Jennie Troup (Digital Music Art)

Syllabus Consultants (Hit Tunes 2018 Repertoire)
Guitar: James Betteridge, Andy G Jones
Bass: Joe Hubbard, Diego Kovadloff, Joel McIver
Drums: Paul Elliott, Pete Riley

Arrangers (Hit Tunes 2018 Repertoire)
Guitar: James Betteridge, Andy G Jones, Mike Goodman, Viv Lock
Bass: Diego Kovadloff, Andy Robertson, Joe Hubbard
Drums: Paul Elliott, Stu Roberts, Pete Riley

Publishing (Hit Tunes 2018 Repertoire)
Fact files by Diego Kovadloff
Covers designed by Phil Millard (Rather Nice design)
Music engraving, internal design and layout by
Simon Troup & Jennie Troup (Digital Music Art)

Distribution
Exclusive Distributors: Hal Leonard

Musicians (Hit Tunes 2018 Repertoire)
Guitar: Andy G Jones, James Betteridge, Mike Goodman,
 David Rhodes (Peter Gabriel)
Bass: Nik Preston, Joe Hubbard, Stuart Clayton,
 Andy Robertson, John Illsley (Dire Straits)
Drums: Paul Elliott, Pete Riley, Peter Huntington, Stu Roberts,
 Billy Cobham (Miles Davis, Mahavishnu Orchestra)
Vocals: Kim Chandler
Keys: Jono Harrison, Hannah V (on 'Red Baron'), Andy Robertson
Horns: Tom Walsh (tpt), Martin Williams (sax), Andy Wood (trmb)

Recording & Audio Engineering (Hit Tunes 2018 Repertoire)
Recording engineers: Oli Jacobs, Scott Barnett, Patrick Phillips
Mixing engineer: Samuel Vasanth
Mastering engineer: Samuel Vasanth
Audio production: Nik Preston
Audio management: Ash Preston, Samuel Vasanth
Recording studios: Real World Studios, The Premises

Publishing (Rockschool 2012 Repertoire)
Fact Files written by Joe Bennett, Charlie Griffiths, Stephen Lawson,
Simon Pitt, Stuart Ryan and James Uings
Walkthroughs written by James Uings
Music engraving, internal design and layout by
Simon Troup & Jennie Troup (Digital Music Art)
Proof reading and copy editing by Chris Bird, Claire Davies, Stephen
Lawson, Simon Pitt and James Uings
Publishing administration by Caroline Uings
Additional drum proof reading by Miguel Andrews

Instrumental Specialists (Rockschool 2012 Repertoire)
Guitar: James Uings
Bass: Stuart Clayton
Drums: Noam Lederman

Musicians (Rockschool 2012 Repertoire)
Andy Crompton, Camilo Tirado, Carl Sterling, Charlie Griffiths,
Chris Webster, Dave Marks, DJ Harry Love, Felipe Karam,
Fergus Gerrand, Henry Thomas, Jake Painter, James Arben,
James Uings, Jason Bowld, Joe Bennett, Jon Musgrave, Kishon Khan,
Kit Morgan, Larry Carlton, Neel Dhorajiwala, Nir Z, Noam Lederman,
Norton York, Richard Pardy, Ross Stanley, Simon Troup, Steve Walker,
Stuart Clayton, Stuart Ryan

Recording & Audio Engineering (Rockschool 2012 Repertoire)
Recorded at The Farm (Fisher Lane Studios)
Produced and engineered by Nick Davis
Assistant engineer and Pro Tools operator Mark Binge
Mixed and mastered at Langlei Studios
Mixing and additional editing by Duncan Jordan
Supporting Tests recorded by Duncan Jordan and Kit Morgan
Mastered by Duncan Jordan
Executive producers: James Uings, Jeremy Ward and Noam Lederman

Executive Producers
John Simpson, Norton York

Table of Contents

Introductions & Information

    1   Title Page
    2   Acknowledgements
    3   Table of Contents
    4   Welcome to Rockschool Guitar Level/Grade 5

Hit Tunes

    5   Eminem — 'Lose Yourself (Live)'
    9   Beyoncé — 'Love On Top'
    13   The Meters — 'People Say'
    17   Average White Band — 'Pick Up the Pieces'
    21   Eric Clapton — 'Lay Down Sally'
    27   AC/DC — 'Hell Ain't A Bad Place To Be'

Rockschool Originals

    33   'Geek'
    39   'Rollin''
    45   'Do Balanço'
    51   'Tiberius'
    57   'Smack Talk'
    63   'Slam Dunk Funk'

Technical Exercises

    69   Scales, Arpeggios, Chords & Riff

Supporting Tests

    72   Sight Reading
    73   Improvisation & Interpretation
    74   Ear Tests
    75   General Musicianship Questions

Additional Information

    76   Marking Schemes
    77   Entering Rockschool Assessments
    77   Mechanical Copyright Information
    78   Introduction to Tone
    80   Guitar Notation Explained

Welcome to Rockschool Guitar Level/Grade 5

Welcome to Guitar Level/Grade 5
Welcome to the **Rockschool 2018 Guitar syllabus**. This book and the accompanying downloadable audio contain everything you need to play guitar at this level/grade. In the book you will find the scores in both standard guitar notation and TAB, as well as Fact Files and Walkthroughs for each song.
The downloadable audio includes:
- full stereo mixes of six Rockschool compositions and six arrangements of classic and contemporary hits
- backing tracks (minus the assessed guitar part)
- all necessary audio for the complete range of supporting tests

Guitar Assessments
At each level/grade, you have the option of taking one of two different types of assessment:

- **Level/Grade Assessment:** a Level/Grade Assessment is a mixture of music performances, technical work and tests. You prepare three pieces (two of which may be Free Choice Pieces) and the contents of the Technical Exercise section. This accounts for 75% of the assessment marks. The other 25% consists of: *either* a Sight Reading *or* an Improvisation & Interpretation test (10%), a pair of instrument specific Ear Tests (10%), and finally you will be asked five General Musicianship Questions (5%). The pass mark is 60%.

- **Performance Certificate:** in a Performance Certificate you play five pieces. Up to three of these can be Free Choice Pieces. Each song is marked out of 20 and the pass mark is 60%.

Book Contents
The book is divided into a number of sections. These are:

- **Assessment Pieces:** in this book you will find six specially commissioned pieces of Level/Grade 5 standard. Each of these is preceded by a *Fact File*. Each Fact File contains a summary of the song, including the style, tempo, key and technical features, along with a list of the musicians who played on it. The song is printed on up to four pages. Immediately after each song is a *Walkthrough*. This covers the song from a performance perspective, focusing on the technical issues you will encounter along the way. Each song comes with a full mix version and a backing track. Both versions have spoken count-ins at the beginning. Please note that any solos played on the full mix versions are indicative only.

- **Technical Exercises:** you should prepare the exercises set in this level/grade in the keys indicated. There is also a Riff test which should be practised and played to the backing track.

- **Supporting Tests and General Musicianship Questions:** in Guitar Level/Grade 5 there are three supporting tests – *either* a Sight Reading *or* an Improvisation & Interpretation test and two Ear Tests – and a set of General Musicianship Questions (GMQs) asked at the end of each assessment. Examples of the types of tests likely to appear in the assessment are printed in this book. Additional examples of both types of test and the GMQs can be found in the Rockschool *Guitar Companion Guide*.

- **Additional Information:** finally, you will find information on assessment procedures, marking schemes, guitar tone, guitar notation, and the full notation and backing track of a piece from the next level/grade as a taster.

Audio
Audio is provided in the form of backing tracks (minus guitar) and examples (including guitar) for the pieces and the supporting tests where applicable. Audio files are supplied in MP3 format to enable playback on a wide range of compatible devices. Digital versions of the book include audio files in the download. Download audio for hardcopy books from RSL directly at *www.rslawards.com/downloads* — you will need to input this code when prompted: **JMDW23X7G6**

Syllabus Guide
All candidates should read the accompanying syllabus guide when using this level/grade book. This can be downloaded from the RSL website: *www.rslawards.com*

Errata
Updates and changes to Rockschool books are documented online. Candidates should check for errata periodically while studying for any assessment. Further details can be found on the RSL website: *www.rslawards.com/errata*

Eminem

SONG TITLE: LOSE YOURSELF
ALBUM: 8 MILE: MUSIC FROM AND INSPIRED BY THE MOTION PICTURE
LABEL: AFTERMATH / INTERSCOPE / WEB
GENRE: HIP HOP

WRITTEN BY: MARSHALL MATHERS
PRODUCED BY: EMINEM, JEFF BASS AND LUIS RESTO

US CHART PEAK: 1

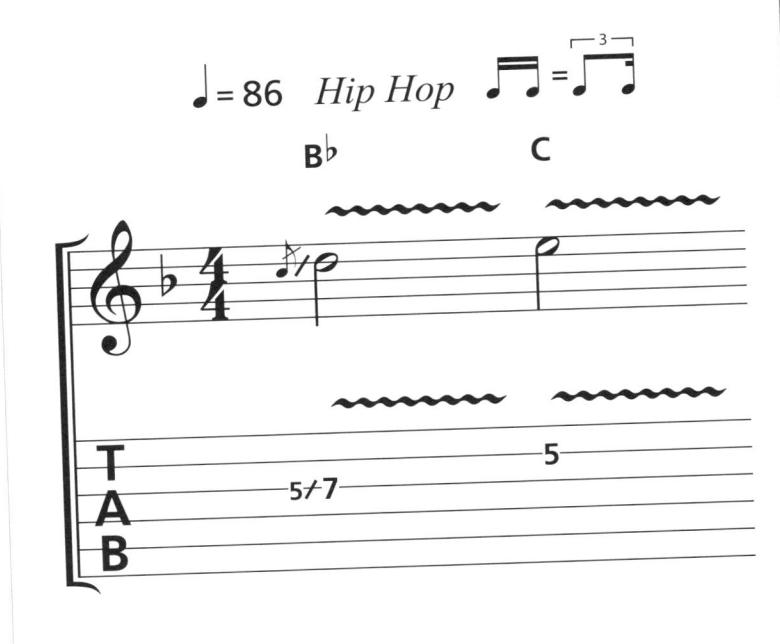

BACKGROUND INFO

'Lose Yourself' was the lead single from the soundtrack to the film *8 Mile* for which Eminem wrote the music and in which he played the character B-Rabbit. The song won an Academy Award for Best Original Song, making it the first rap song to receive the accolade. 'Lose Yourself' has received widespread critical acclaim for its lyrical content, rapping and production styles. The lyrics are a departure for Eminem, delivering a hard-hitting tale of self-reflection and insight, exploring themes such as being in the moment, losing one's self in the power of music and seizing opportunity and achieving what is wished by setting one's mind to it.

The song sold over 10 million copies in the US alone. Eminem wrote it whilst on set and recorded it on a portable studio in one take. The sheet on which he wrote the lyrics for 'Lose Yourself' appear in the movie during a scene in which B-Rabbit is writing whilst riding on a bus. 'Lose Yourself' topped the Billboard Hot 100 charts spending 12 weeks at no. 1 and a total of 16 in the Top Ten.

'Lose Yourself' was produced by Eminen in partnership with Jeff Bass, one half of the Bass Brothers production duo, who played guitars on the recording. Jeff Bass signed a contract with Quincy Jones aged 19 and has since become one of the most successful producers in the music industry. The Bass Brothers have worked with George Clinton P Funk and were very significant in the development of Eminem's career.

Eminem's lyrics sparked much controversy due to their alleged misogynistic and nihilistic views and Eminem himself has acknowledged his views are controversial. There is also a directness and honesty in much of what he talks about, including financial hardship and feeling out of place from a young age, that makes his music connect with many people. Despite the serious subjects his lyrics touch upon, they have also been acknowledged as humorous by many and that creates inevitable appeal.

Eminem has released nine records to date and has also acted in the film *The Interview*. He published his biography, *The Way I Am*, in 2008. His *Revival* Tour of 2018 saw him perform in arenas and stadiums. Eminem has sold over 100 million records worldwide.

Lose Yourself (Live)

Eminem

Words & Music by Marshall Mathers,
Jeff Bass & Luis Resto

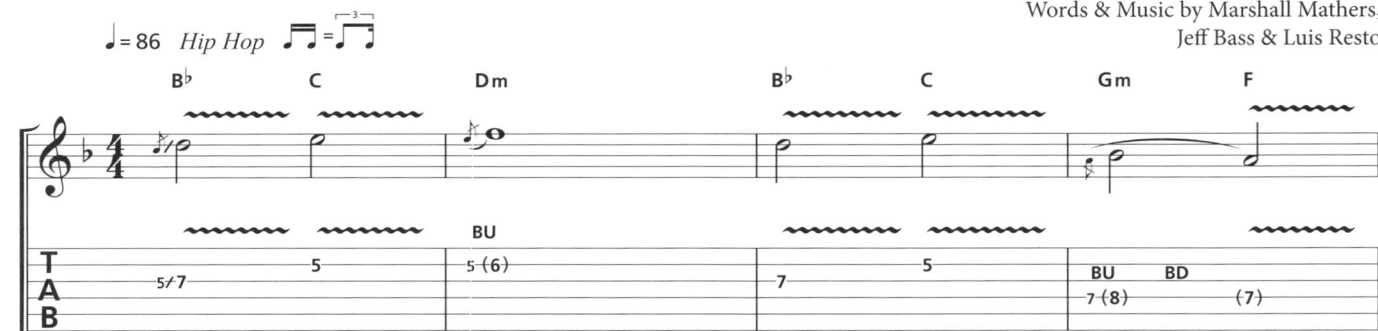

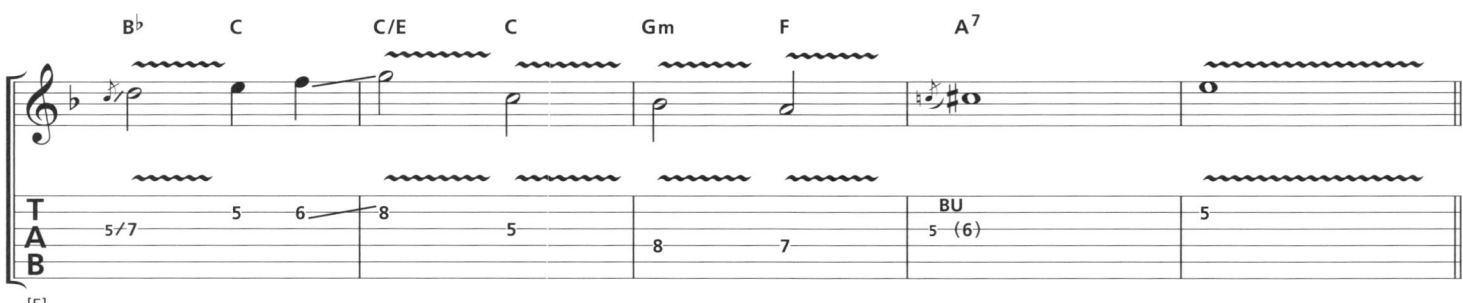

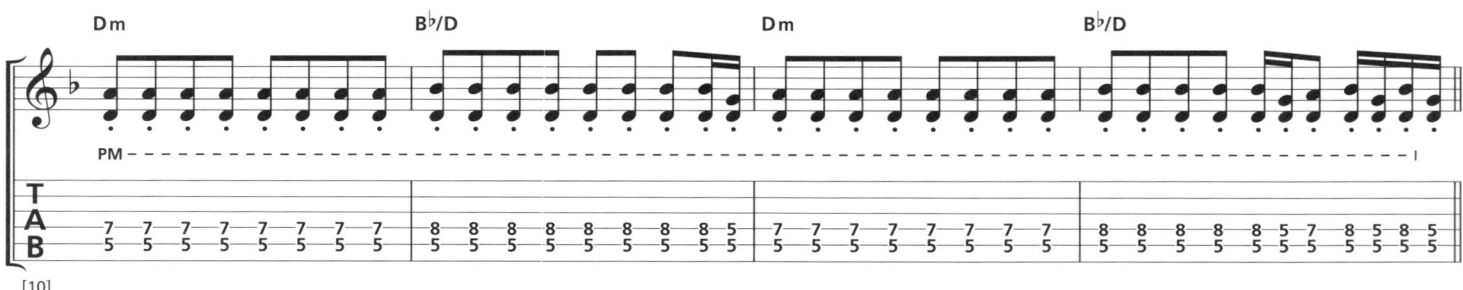

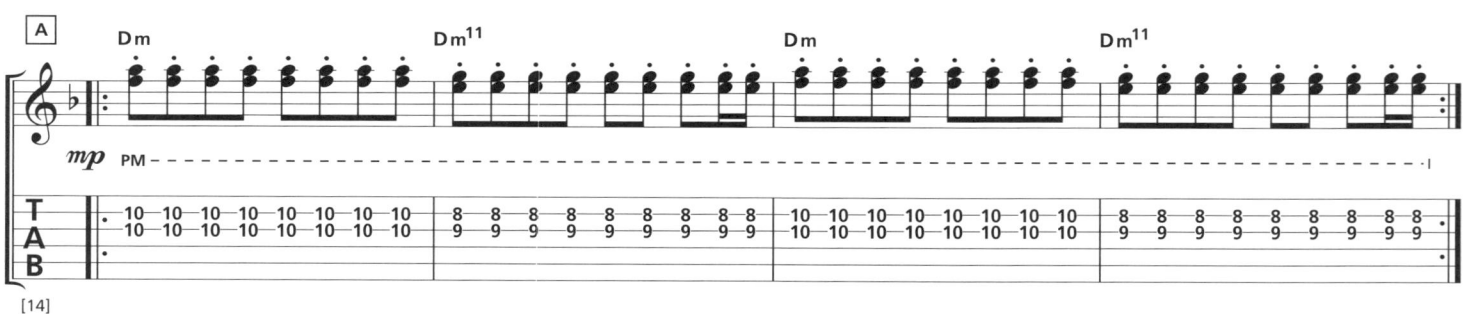

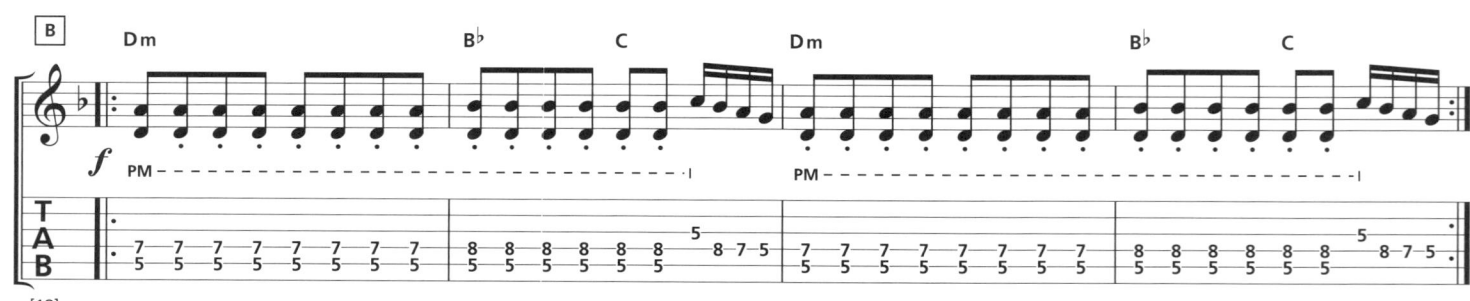

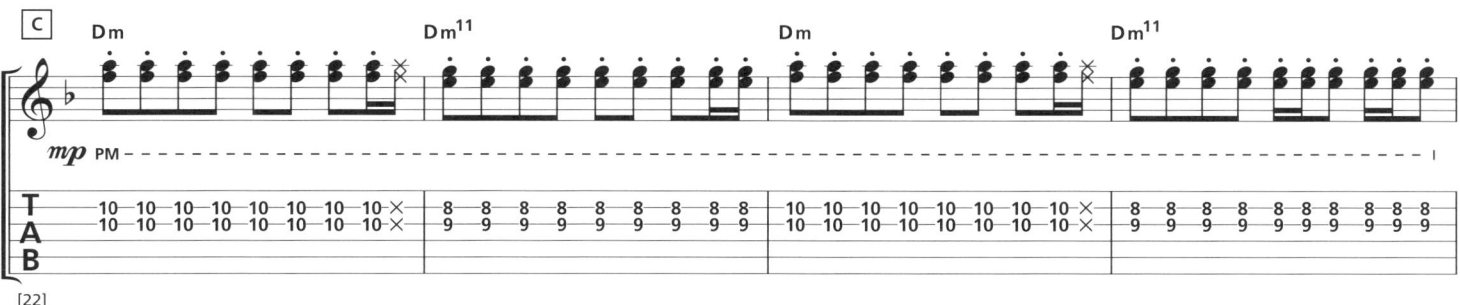

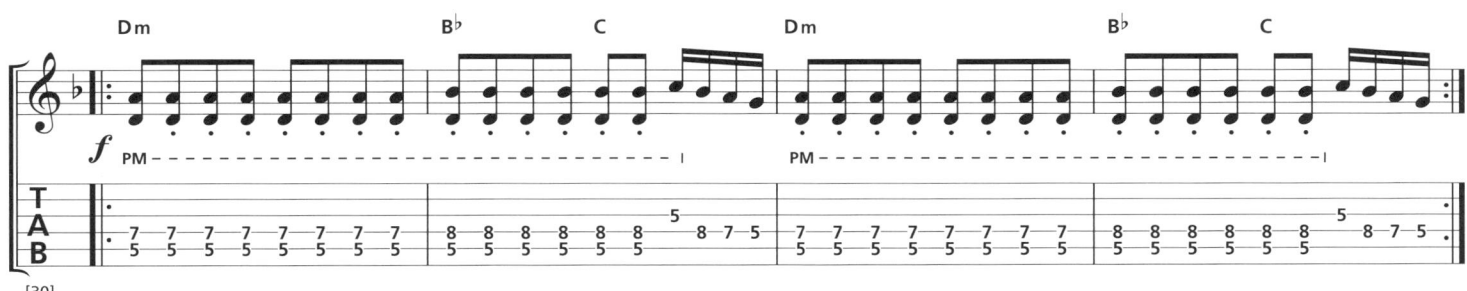
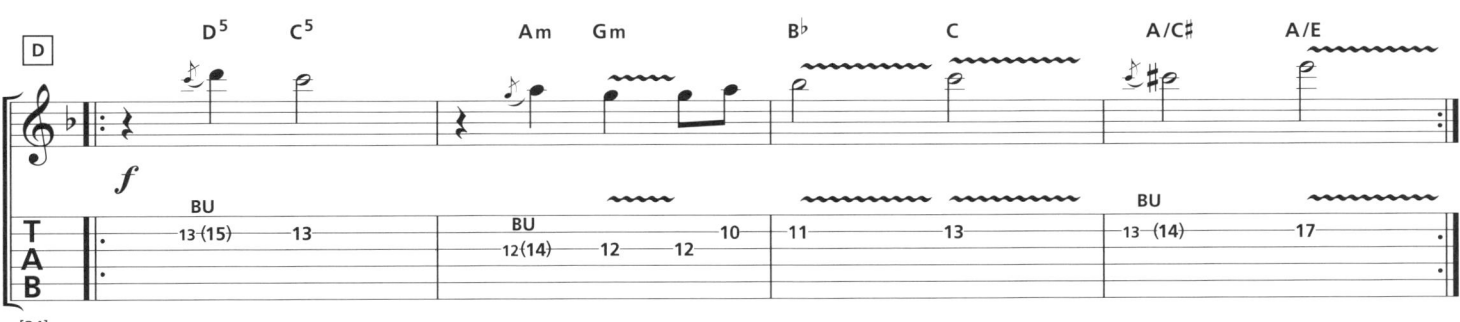
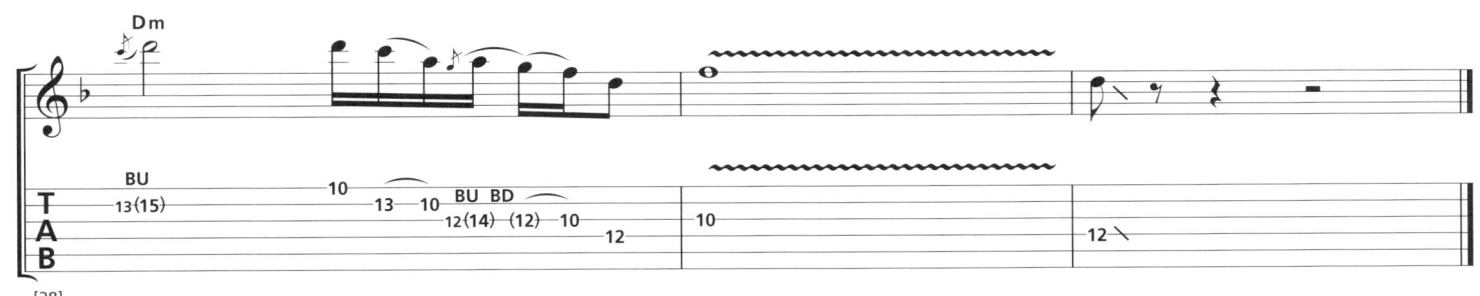

Walkthrough

Amp Settings

There are two main sounds required to play this song – a mixture of a slightly overdriven sound for the Verse and Chorus riffs, and a heavily overdriven sound for the intro, Verse 2 (C section) and outro single note melodies. The song was recorded on a Stratocaster style guitar using both the bridge and middle pickup.

Note that the amp EQ settings are just suggestions and its worth experimenting with the levels of Bass, Middle and Treble and see what you prefer.

Depending on the guitar and amplifier you play through these settings will change, so it's important to become familiar and experiment with all the controls on your guitar, and find tonal 'colours' that you like and feel are suitable for different styles and genres of music that you want to play.

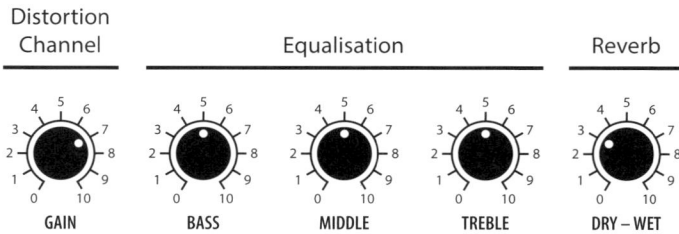

Intro

The song starts with a subtle atmospheric melodic line to set up the main groove of the song. The song is in the key of D minor with the chords moving from $B\flat^{(\flat6)}$ to C^7 then to D minor (i). Notice the variations in the harmony in measure 4, where the chords move from G minor (iv) to F (III), then in measure 6, with the C/E (1st inversion C major chord) The challenge with the intro is to concentrate on note lengths, accurate semitone bends, and consistent vibrato. The chord sequence ends on an A^7 (V) chord, setting up the entrance of the main riff. The main riff is based around the chords D minor to $B\flat/D$ (1st inversion $B\flat$), with the guitar playing D^5 (D and A), then raising the A on the D string to a $B\flat$, creating a $\sharp5/\flat6$ interval from the D, giving the riff an unsettled, dramatic feel.

A Section (Verse)

In the A section the guitar plays a variation on the main riff, playing F ($\flat$3rd) and A (5th) on the G and B string over the D minor chord, then G (11th) and E (9th) over the Dm^{11} chord. Focus on the swung feel of the riff, accenting the first eighth note on each down beat.

B Section (Chorus)

The B section returns to the main riff for the chorus, with a descending melodic figure embellishment in measures 19 and 21.

C Section (Verse)

In the C section the guitar plays the same verse figure from section A, but from measure 26 the guitar plays a melodic single note figure over the second half of the verse based around the D minor pentatonic scale, leading back into the chorus (D section).

D Section (Outro)

The guitar in the D section plays in unison with bass and drums, with a melodic line based around the D minor pentatonic scale, with a semitone bend from the $\flat7$ to a major 7th interval in measure 37, hinting a harmonic minor 'flavour'. The song ends with a pentatonic lick ending on the penultimate measure where the guitar hangs on the minor 3rd (F) before resolving to the tonic (D) on beat 1 of the last measure.

If you are struggling with any parts in the song try isolating the measures that you want to focus on and practice them in isolation without the backing track. It may also help to play along with just a metronome to help focus on the areas that may need attention. Playing along with just a metronome will help develop good time and help develop your 'inner clock'.

Beyoncé

SONG TITLE: LOVE ON TOP
ALBUM: 4
LABEL: COLUMBIA
GENRE: R&B

WRITTEN BY: BEYONCÉ KNOWLES, TERIUS NASH AND SHEA TAYLOR
PRODUCED BY: BEYONCÉ KNOWLES AND SHEA TAYLOR

US CHART PEAK: 20

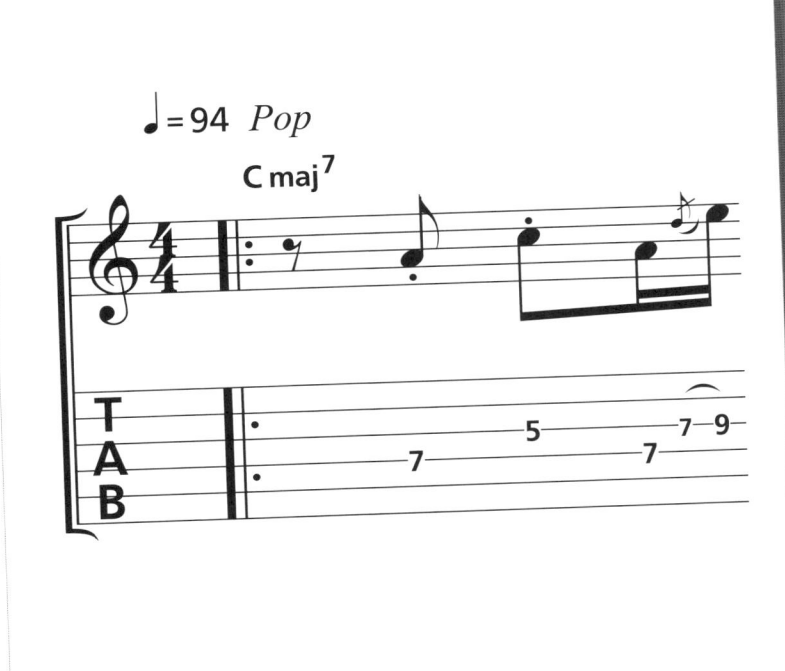

BACKGROUND INFO

'Love On Top' was released as a single in September 2011 and was featured on Beyoncé's fourth studio album *4*. The single reached the top of the R&B/Hip-Hop Songs chart and remained in that position for seven weeks. 'Love On Top' signified a stylistic departure for Beyoncé. She was inspired by her feelings whilst playing Etta James in the film *Cadillac Records*. Beyoncé's delivery style is rawer and more direct than in previous recordings and her lyrics reflect a new kind of introspection in her writing. The main theme of the song is reliance. The portrayal of Etta James gave Beyoncé a new-found confidence to be bolder and stronger in her music. In 'Love On Top' Beyoncé displays phenomenal vocal versatility. The song has four key changes in the end section and this garnered much attention particularly when critics saw she could perform it live at ease. Beyoncé has a four octave range.

'Love On Top' was written by Beyoncé, Terius Nash and Shea Taylor, and produced by Beyoncé in partnership with Shea Taylor. The style of the song surprised critics and commentators because it has a 1980s retro feel, paying dues to the style of Stevie Wonder, Anita Baker, and Whitney Houston. The single sold over 5 million copies worldwide.

The guitarists that recorded on the album session were Pat Thrall and Robert R.T. Taylor. Thrall is a seasoned session player from the 1970s, who established an association with many R&B producers in the 1990s, and has worked with Rihanna, Justin Bieber, and Jessie J amongst many others. Taylor is also an experienced player, with much live experience on the R&B scene, whose credits include Ne-Yo and Janet Jackson.

Beyoncé Knowles was born in Houston, Texas, in 1981. She performed and sang from a young age and in the late 1990s rose to fame as the lead singer of R&B girl group Destiny's Child with whom she sold 60 million records. Beyoncé's voice and singing style are distinctive and powerful.

During a break with the band in 2003 she released *Dangerously in Love*. The record was an immediate success, selling 12 million copies and earning five Grammy Awards. Her solo career continued to grow and she has now sold approximately 120 million records.

Love On Top

Beyoncé

Words & Music by Terius Nash,
Beyoncé Knowles & Robert Taylor

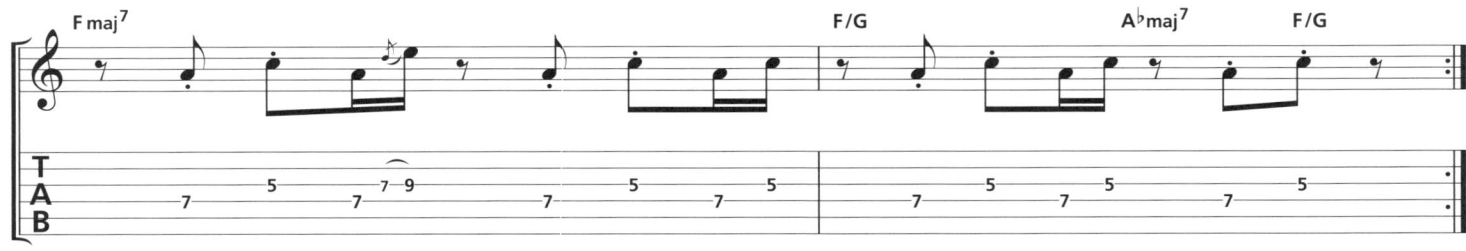
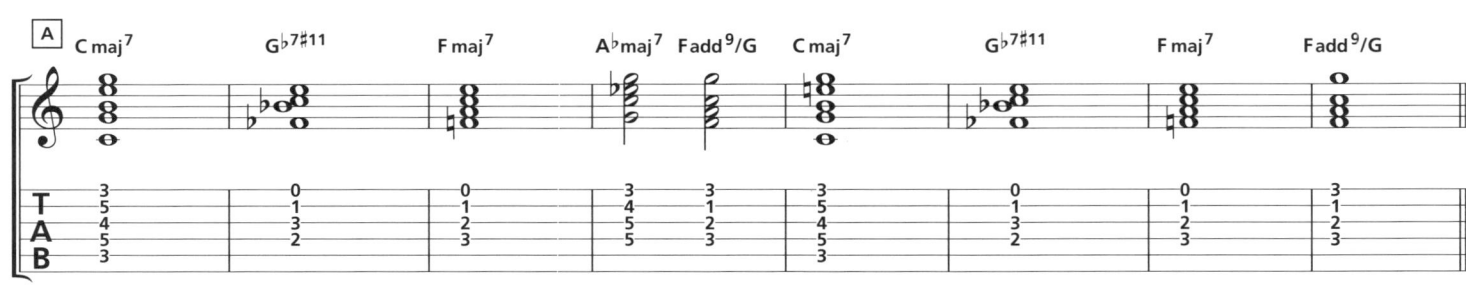
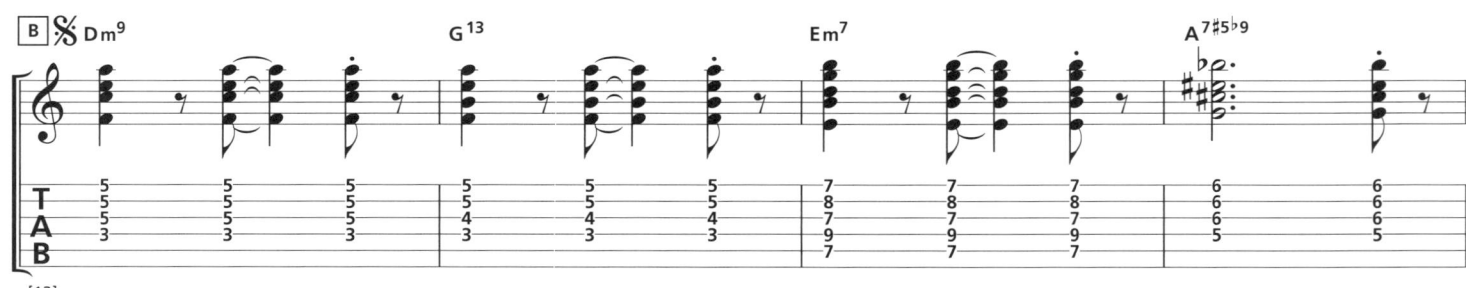
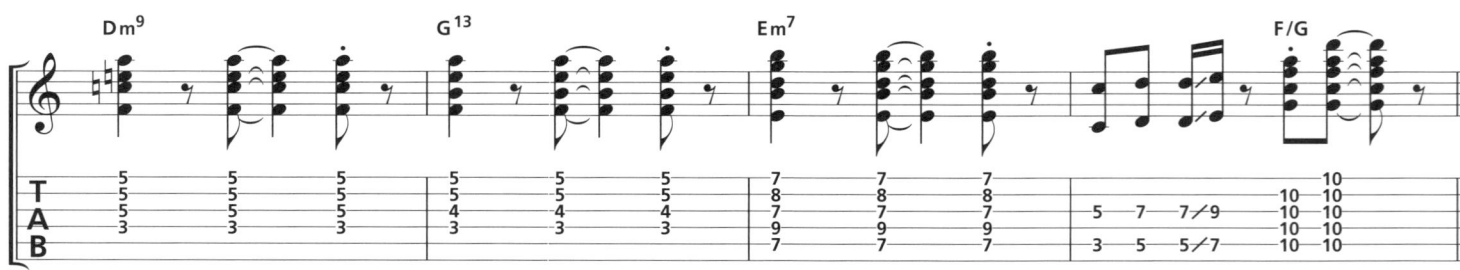
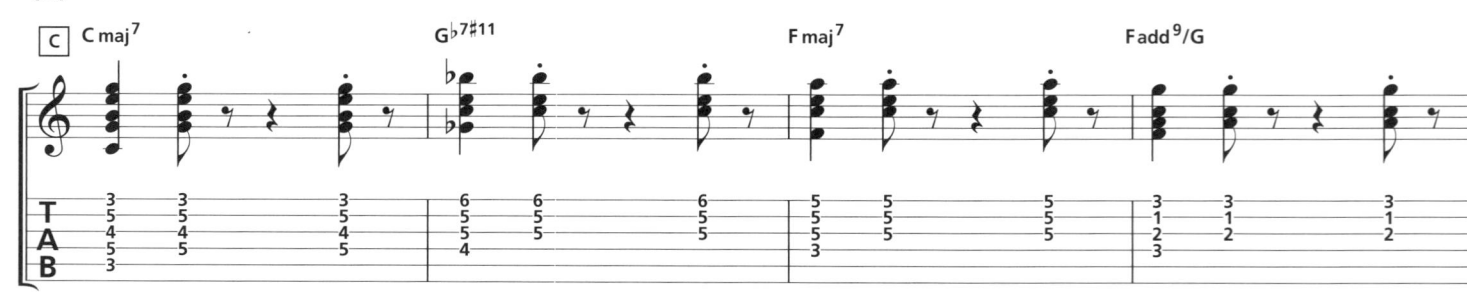

© Copyright 2011 Music Publishing/B Day Publishing/DLJ Songs/EMI April Music Incorporated.
EMI Music Publishing Limited/Warner/Chappell North America Limited/Downtown Music UK Limited.
All Rights Reserved. International Copyright Secured.

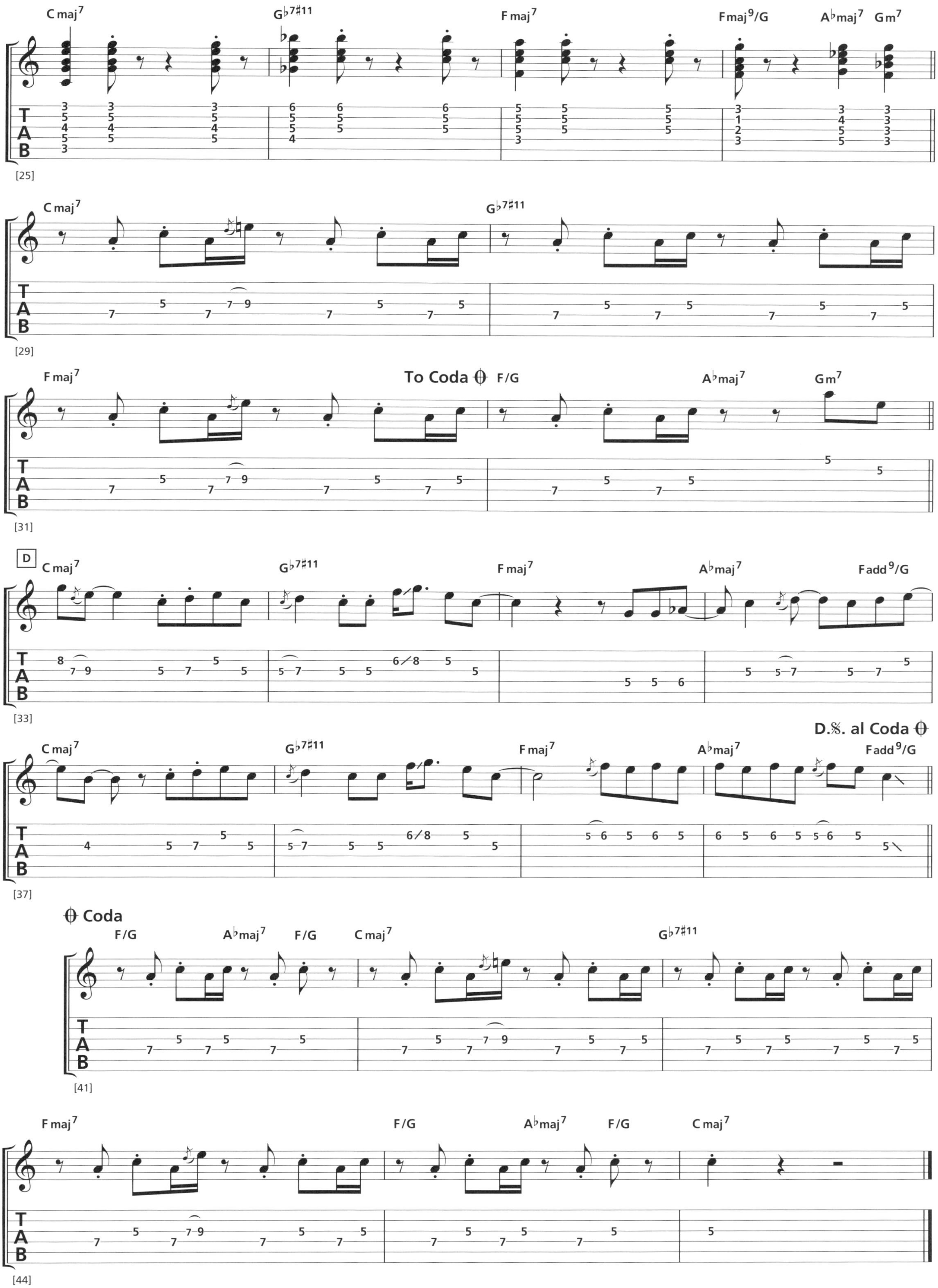
C maj7
G♭7♯11
F maj7
Fmaj9/G
A♭maj7
Gm7
[25]
[29]
To Coda
F/G
[31]
D
Fadd9/G
[33]
D.𝄋. al Coda
[37]
Coda
[41]
[44]

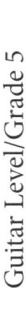

Walkthrough

Amp Settings

There are two main sounds required for this song – the intro riff and solo section are played through an overdriven/distorted sound, with the verse and chorus sections played through a clean sound. Practise changing between sounds, making sure that the volume levels on both the clean and dirty channels are set accordingly.

Note that these settings are just suggestions and, depending on the guitar and amplifier you play through, these settings will change. Experiment with pickup selection and tone settings on your guitar to see what different tonal colours you like and feel suit the sound of the song the best.

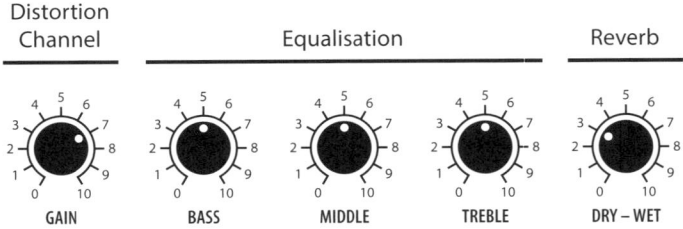

Intro

The intro starts with a single note riff based around the C major pentatonic scale, moving between an A (major 6th) and a C (tonic) with an E (major 3rd) in the 1st, and 3rd measures.

A Section (Verse)

The guitar in the A section plays long chords, moving through the changes $Cmaj^7$ (I), $G\flat^{7(\sharp 11)}$ ($\flat$V), $Fmaj^7$ (IV), before moving from an $A\flat maj^7$ ($\flat$3), then $Fadd^9/G$. Some of these chords may look a little daunting to begin with, as well as the chord progression itself. Analysing chord progressions will give you a better understanding of harmony in general, which in turn will provide you with a better understanding of how different scales work over different chord types and different chord progressions. A good tip when beginning to analyse chord progressions is to simplify any 'complicated' chords by ignoring any extensions to begin with. If we do this we are left with the chords C major, C^7, F major, $A\flat$ major, F major.

Harmonised C major scale:

I	ii	iii	IV	V	vi	vii
$Cmaj^7$	Dm^7	Em^7	$Fmaj^7$	G^7	Am^7	$Bm^{7\flat 5}$

So, we can see that the C major, F major and G major are the I, IV and V of the scale.

So what about the $A\flat$ major and the $G\flat^{7(\sharp 11)}$?

The $A\flat maj^7$ chord has been 'borrowed' from the parallel key of C minor (VI).

Harmonised C Natural minor:

i	ii	III	iv	v	VI	VII
Cm^7	$Dm^{7\flat 5}$	$E\flat maj^7$	Fm^7	Gm^7	$A\flat maj^7$	$B\flat^7$

The $G\flat^{7(\sharp 11)}$ can be seen as a tri-tone substitution of C^7 (secondary dominant of F major in the key of C). A tri-tone substitution is when a dominant chord is substituted for another 7th chord that is a tri-tone (3 whole tones) away from the original chord.

B Section (Bridge)

The guitar in the B section plays Dm^9 (ii of C major) to G^{13} (V of C major), before moving to Em^7 (iii) then $A^{7(\sharp 5\flat 9)}$ which provides a really strong resolution (perfect cadence) back to the Dm^9 chord. In the last measure the guitar plays an F/G (V of C major), which again provides a perfect cadence into the chorus (section C).

C Section Chorus

The guitar in the C section plays the same chord progression as the A section, but with a more involved rhythm figure. The main accents are on the back beat, (beats 2 and 4) with a quarter note on beat 1. Work on getting the change from playing the long notes (beat 1) to playing the short staccato notes on beats 2 and 4 consistently.

D Section solo

The D section is a solo based on the top line melody Beyoncé sings on the original track. The solo is based predominantly around the C major pentatonic scale, with other intervals from the major scale included for extra 'flavour' in areas. A good example of this is in measure 37 where the guitar lands on the note B (major 7th of the $Cmaj^7$ chord). Can you identify any others? At the end of the solo take the *D.S.*, back to the beginning of the B section, until the *To Coda* sign at measure 31.

Coda.

The guitar returns to the single note figure played in the intro to finish the song, ending on a C on beat 1 of the last measure.

The Meters

SONG TITLE: PEOPLE SAY
ALBUM: REJUVENATION
LABEL: REPRISE
GENRE: FUNK

WRITTEN BY: ART NEVILLE,
ZIGABOO MODELISTE,
LEO NOCENTELLI
AND GEORGE PORTER JR.
PRODUCED BY: ALLEN TOUSSAINT
AND THE METERS

US CHART PEAK: 52

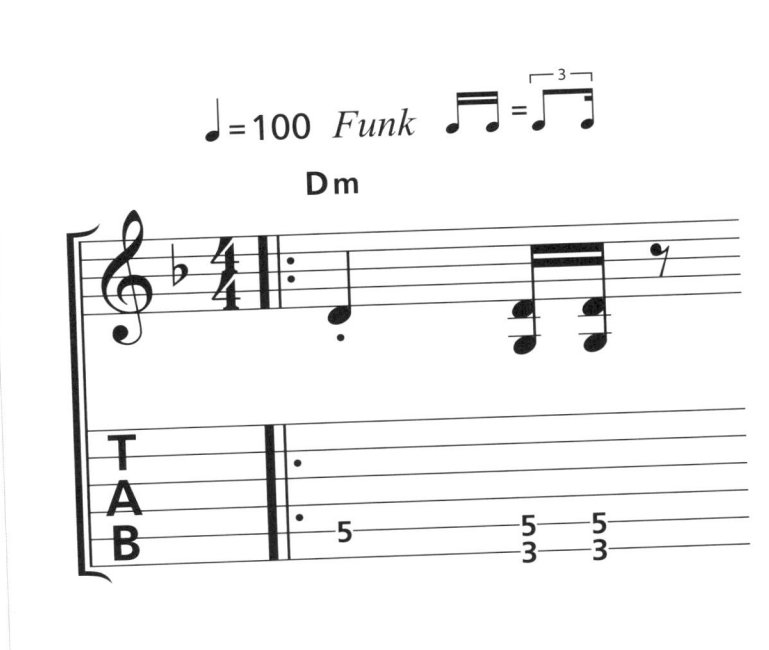

BACKGROUND INFO

'People Say' is featured on The Meters' *Rejuvenation* album, their first recording for the Reprise label, released in July 1974. The album signals a change in The Meters' approach to their songs, including more lead vocals featuring lyrics with a social connotation, as is the case in 'People Say'. *Rejuvenation* showcases The Meters at the peak of their powers, driving forth a unique blend of New Orleans funk and swamp rock that sets the band apart and makes them immediately identifiable. By 1974 the funk genre was well established in the mainstream but there were few artists that could claim to be original creators of a sound and style. The Meters are regarded as the originators of funk together with James Brown.

The Meters formed in 1965 in New Orleans. The group featured Zigaboo Modeliste on drums, George Porter Jr. on bass, Art Neville on keyboards and Leo Nocentelli on guitar, who were later joined by Cyril Neville on percussion and vocals. The Meters worked as house band for the Sansu Enterprises record label, owned by Allen Toussaint who would produce seven of their eight albums between 1969 and 1977. The Meters recorded successful and highly influential songs, such as 'Sophisticated Cissy', 'Look-Ka Py Py' and 'Chicken Strut' and later collaborated with many other musicians such as Dr. John, Paul McCartney, King Biscuit Boy, Labelle and Robert Palmer amongst others. They also kept a busy live schedule. In 1975 Paul McCartney invited them to play aboard the Queen Mary at the release party for his album *Venus and Mars*. Mick Jagger was in attendance and was so impressed with the band that he invited them to open for The Rolling Stones on their American tour in 1975 and their European tour in 1976. In 1977 Art and Cyril Neville left the band, prompting Porter to do so later in that year. Although they were replaced by other musicians by 1980 The Meters had officially broken up.

Leo Nocentelli is regarded as significant guitarist in the history of funk and other associated styles. He has performed in various quartets under his musical leadership and continues to this day. His list of collaborations include Al Di Meola, Oteil Burbridge, Patti LaBelle, Peter Gabriel, Etta James, Robbie Robertson, Maceo Parker and Trombone Shorty amongst many others.

People Say

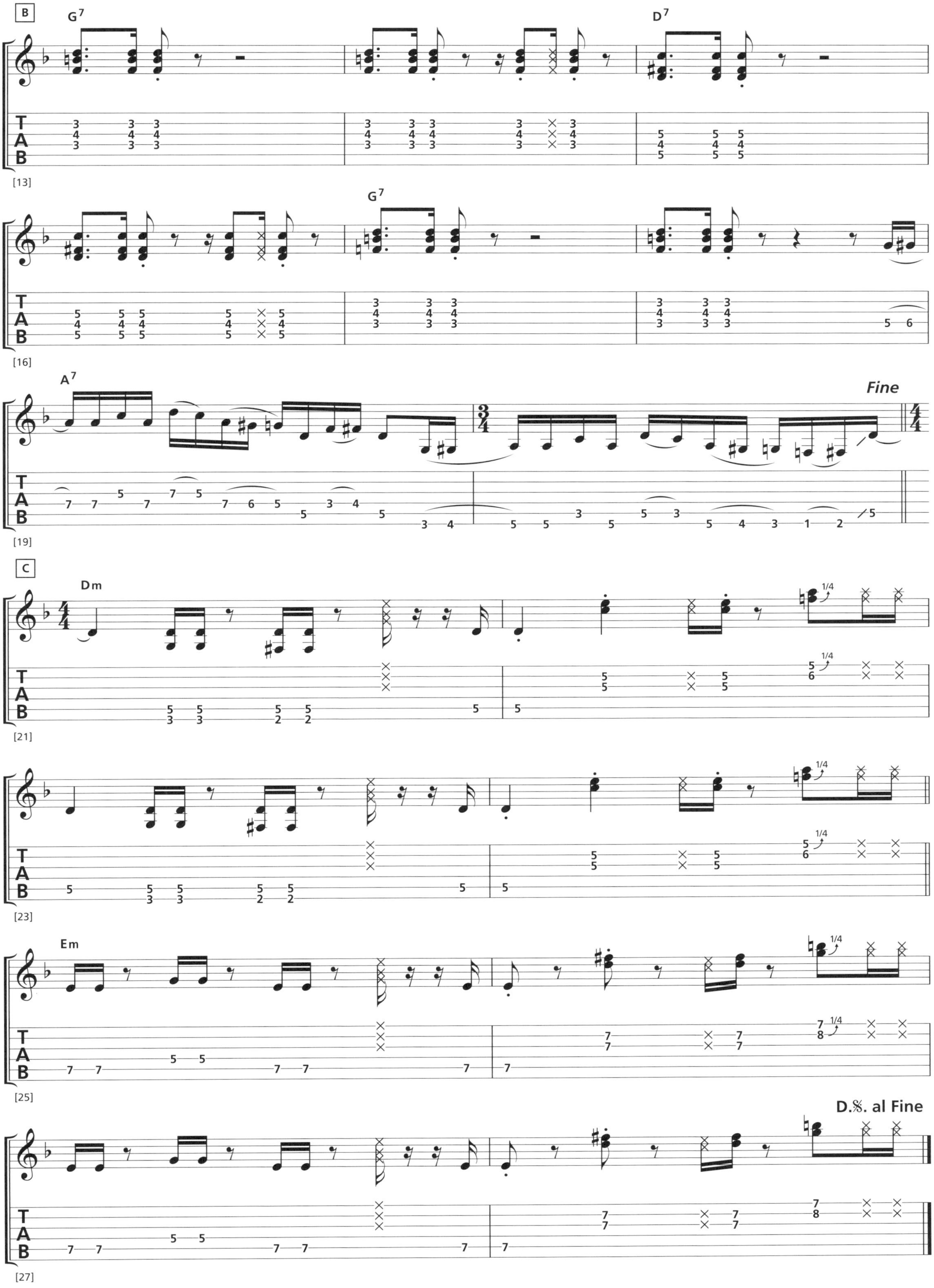
B
G7
D7
[13]
G7
[16]
A7
Fine
[19]
C
Dm
1/4
[21]
[23]
Em
[25]
D.𝄋. al Fine
[27]
TAB

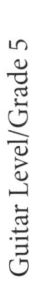

Walkthrough

Amp Settings

A clean sound with a small amount of drive/gain is required for this song. The track was recorded on a Stratocaster style guitar played on the neck pickup (pickup nearest the neck of the guitar). Note the amp settings are just suggestions. Depending on the guitar and amplifier you play through these settings will change. Experiment with pickup selection and tone settings on your guitar to see what different tonal 'colours' you like and feel suit the sound of the song the best.

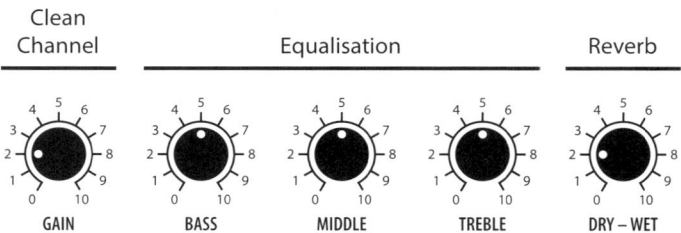

Intro

The Intro begins with a guitar riff based around a D^9 chord. In measure 1 the riff moves between the 4th (G) and major 3rd (F#), and in measure 2 plays the ♭7 (C), and the 9th (E) with a quarter note bend on the minor 3rd (F). From measure 5 the guitar plays a variation on the opening riff with the overall tonality shifting to a minor feel. The riff moves between the root (D) and the minor 3rd (F) on the 5th and 4th strings in measure 1, with measure 2 playing the same figure as the opening riff. Spend time becoming comfortable with the 16th-note rhythm, and articulation with moving between the fretted and muted notes.

A Section (Verse)

The A section continues with the same riff for eight measures (take note of the repeat at measure 12).

B Section (Chorus)

The B section moves between a G^7 (V) to a D^7 (I7) chord. Notice the small chord clusters, (root, major 3rd, and ♭7th). Work on left and right hand muting to avoid catching any unwanted strings. Focus on practising moving your strumming hand in time with the underlying 16th-note subdivision. The B section ends with a unison (played together) line played by both bass and guitar, outlining the A^7 and D^7 chords. Watch out for the ¾ measure at measure 20, leading back into the main riff at section C.

C Section

The song returns to the beginning riff, before modulating up a whole step to E minor for four measures, before returning back to D minor Take the *D.S. al Fine* back to the beginning of section A and play through to the fine sign at the end of the unison line at measure 20.

If you are struggling with any parts in the song try isolating the measures that you want to focus on and practice them in isolation without the backing track. It may also help to play along with just a metronome to help focus on the areas that may need attention. Playing along with just a metronome will help you develop good time and help develop your 'inner clock'.

Average White Band

SONG TITLE: PICK UP THE PIECES
ALBUM: AWB
LABEL: ATLANTIC
GENRE: FUNK / JAZZ FUNK

WRITTEN BY: ROGER BALL, MALCOLM DUNCAN, ALAN GORRIE, ONNIE MCINTYRE, HAMISH STUART AND ROBBIE MCINTOSH
PRODUCED BY: ARIF MARDIN

US CHART PEAK: 1

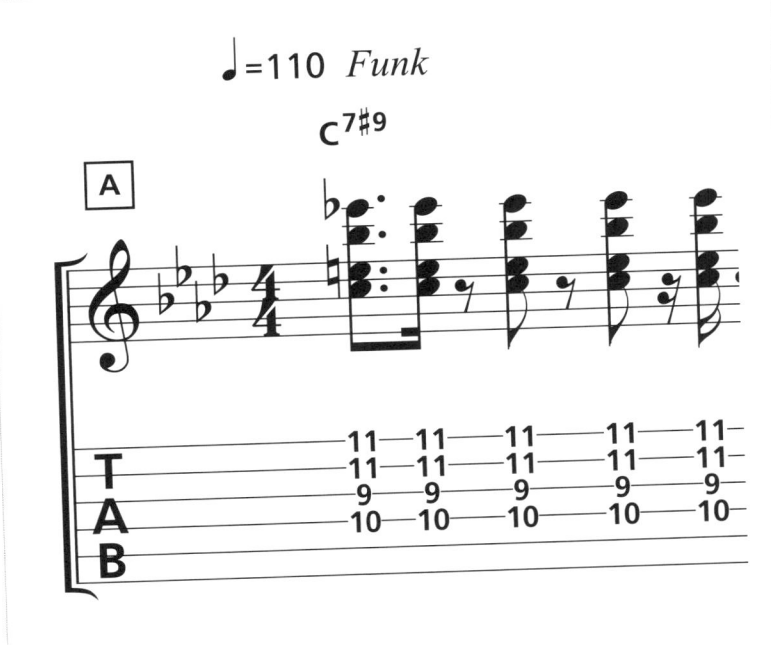

BACKGROUND INFO

'Pick Up The Pieces' was written collaboratively by the Average White Band and produced by Arif Mardin who initially disagreed with releasing it as a single. Saxophonist Malcolm Duncan claims Mardin thought that "a funk instrumental played by Scotsmen with no lyrics other than a shout" was going to get nowhere. He was proved wrong – 'Pick Up The Pieces' reached the top of the Singles Chart in the US and *AWB*, the band's debut album featuring the song, topped the US Album charts. After its success in the US, 'Pick Up The Pieces' charted in the UK having initially failed to do so. According to Duncan the "pick up the pieces" shouts were a relevant call to pick oneself up when things were not going well.

The Average White Band formed in London in early 1972. All members hailed from Scotland and had occasionally played together there but upon meeting by chance at a Traffic concert, they decided to start jamming together. A friend heard them and allegedly remarked "this is too much for the average white man". They liked the phrase and used it as a name. In 1973 the band released their debut album *Show Your Hand* but it sold poorly. They did, however, manage to secure a support slot for Eric Clapton's comeback concert. Bruce McCaskill, who managed Clapton at the time, liked them and agreed to manage them. He borrowed money and took them to the US to promote their music. McCaskill had a vast network there and managed to sign them to Atlantic. The band relocated to Los Angeles where they recorded *AWB* with renowned producer Arif Mardin. Shortly after the record was completed drummer Robbie McIntosh died of a heroin overdose whilst at Cher's house and was replaced by Steve Ferrone, who remained with band.

In 1975 the Average White Band released *Cut The Cake*, dedicated to Robbie McIntosh. It was followed by *Soul Searching* in 1976. Both records where commercially successful and yielded Top 40 hits. A string of records followed until the band decided to go their separate ways in 1983.

Hamish Stuart, who played guitar, bass and sung in the band, joined Paul McCartney's band in 1989 and worked with him until 1993.

Pick Up the Pieces

Average White Band

Music by Roger Ball, Alan Gorrie, Malcolm Duncan, Robert McIntosh, Owen McIntyre & James Stuart

© Copyright 1972 Average Music/Joe's Songs.
Fairwood Music Limited/BMG Rights Management (US) LLC/Wixen Music UK Limited.
All Rights Reserved. International Copyright Secured.

Walkthrough

Amp Settings

To capture this classic funk guitar sound, a completely clean tone would be best. If you have the choice, a suitable amp or amp model would be 'American clean' (or equivalent), and a little compression would be help the overall presentation. If you use a three pickup guitar, position four (the middle and bridge pickups mixed) might be best.

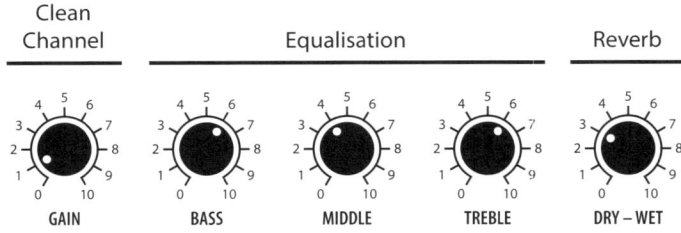

Intro Section (Measures 1–4)

This is one of the most iconic intro guitar parts in all of funk music – quite impressive for a group of guys from Scotland!

Measure 1

This is a classic $C^{7\sharp9}$ voicing which is sometimes referred to as 'The Jimi Hendrix chord' after his guitar part on the classic 'Purple Haze'. The other defining factor of this intro part is the rhythm. If you're unfamiliar with this kind of rhythm it would be worth taking the time to carefully figure out where the notes fall on a 'grid' of 16ths.

The chords fall on beat 1, the 'a' of beat 1, the 'and' of beat 2, the 'and' of beat 3 and the 'e' of beat 4. Remember the beats are counted "1, e, &, a, 2, e, &, a, 3, e, &, a, 4, e, &, a". Please bear in mind the importance of learning and absorbing the sound and feel of these subdivisions – you are essentially training your mind to recognise these patterns. The more carefully you study them, the quicker you will have them at your disposal.

A Section (Measures 5–18)

This is a hugely influential rhythm part. It's a syncopated 16th-note extravaganza! Again, the key to mastering this is to patiently decipher the rhythms.

Measure 5

This measure clearly states the underlying Fm^7 harmony. The line is mostly based around the F minor pentatonic scale, however, the chromatic move from $E\flat$–E natural moving onto F in the next measure is a common idea in funk music. Without going into huge detail bebop jazz players would claim this as their own.

Measure 9

This is a variation on the theme of measure 5. The new development is the addition of the ear-catching skip up to $E\flat$.

Measure 13

Here the idea from measure 5 is repeated over the $B\flat^7$ chord. This is a core feature of chordal voicings in funk music – notice that we only change the notes that need to be changed in order to avoid clashing with the harmony.

B Section (Measures 19–23)

This is a contrasting section, the rhythm recalls the opening riff but over the $B\flat^7$ harmony. Again this is a characteristically syncopated funk part. Keep your right wrist loose but be careful to really feel the pulse. Try to tap your foot along with the beat in order to anchor your rhythmic placement. Always have the grid of 16th subdivisions visualised in your head.

Guitar Solo Section (Measures 34–37 repeated)

Here the harmony is $B\flat^9$ – try using $B\flat$ Mixolydian on this chord (See Fig. 1). Experiment with the backing track. You could try adding a touch of $B\flat$ blues in there. If you're a fairly experienced improviser the $B\flat$ bebop scale is definitely an option. The bebop scale is created when you add the major 7th degree as a passing note to the Mixolydian mode.

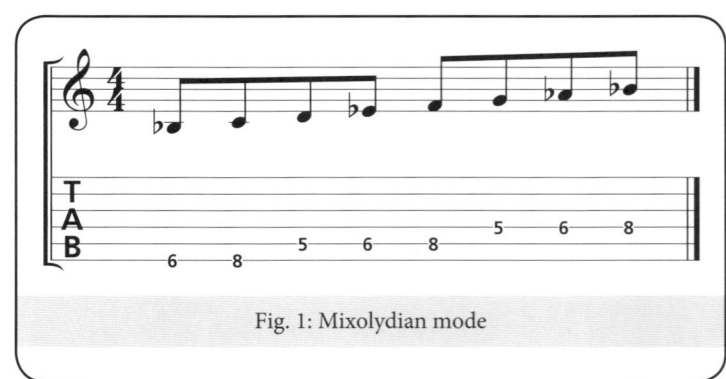

Fig. 1: Mixolydian mode

Eric Clapton

SONG TITLE: LAY DOWN SALLY
ALBUM: SLOWHAND
LABEL: RSO
GENRE: ROOTS ROCK / COUNTRY ROCK

WRITTEN BY: MARCELLA DETROIT AND GEORGE TERRY
PRODUCED BY: GLYN JOHNS

US CHART PEAK: 3

BACKGROUND INFO

'Lay Down Sally' was released in November 1977 and was a crossover country hit, influenced by the style of J.J. Cale, whom Eric Clapton greatly admires. The recording featured the song's co-writer Marcella Detroit and very well-respected musicians such as Carl Radle on bass, Jamie Oldaker on drums, Dick Sims on electric piano and George Terry on guitar. *Slowhand*, the album featuring 'Lay Down Sally', was produced by Glyn Johns who by 1977 had produced and engineered seminal records in rock's history for artists including The Beatles, The Rolling Stones, The Who, The Faces and The Eagles. Johns is famed for his unique approach to the recording of drums. *Slowhand* yielded the hit 'Wonderful Tonight'. Clapton and Johns joined forces again in 2016 for the recording of Clapton's twenty-third album *I Still Do*.

Eric Clapton is regarded as one of rock and roll's most important guitarists and is amongst a small group of instrumentalists who became the blueprint for aspiring lead guitarists. He favoured many guitars during his time but he eventually settled for 'Blackie', a Fender Stratocaster made from three different guitars. With Cream he used a Gibson Les Paul Standard. The guitar was stolen and he bought a replacement from Andy Summers (later of The Police) who had a nearly identical one. Eric Clapton performed and recorded with The Yardbirds, John Mayall's Bluesbreakers, Cream, Blind Faith and Derek and The Dominos before embarking on a highly successful solo career that yielded hit singles such as 'Layla', 'I Shot The Sheriff', 'Cocaine' and 'Tears In Heaven'.

Eric Clapton was an advanced player by the age of 16 and his fluid and lyrical blues based delivery has been admired and imitated all over the world. In a career spanning over 50 years he has played with a 'who's who' of the popular music world and toured all over the planet. Clapton has played the Royal Albert Hall over 200 times. His career has been marred by personal tragedy and addiction. After many struggles with drink and drugs he managed to sober up and in 1998 he established the Crossroads Centre in Antigua, specialising in helping drug and alcohol addicts.

Eric Clapton is the recipient of 18 Grammy Awards and has sold nearly 130 million records worldwide.

Lay Down Sally

Eric Clapton
Words & Music by Eric Clapton,
George Terry & Marcy Levy

© Copyright 1977 & 1999 Throat Music Limited.
All Rights Reserved. International Copyright Secured.

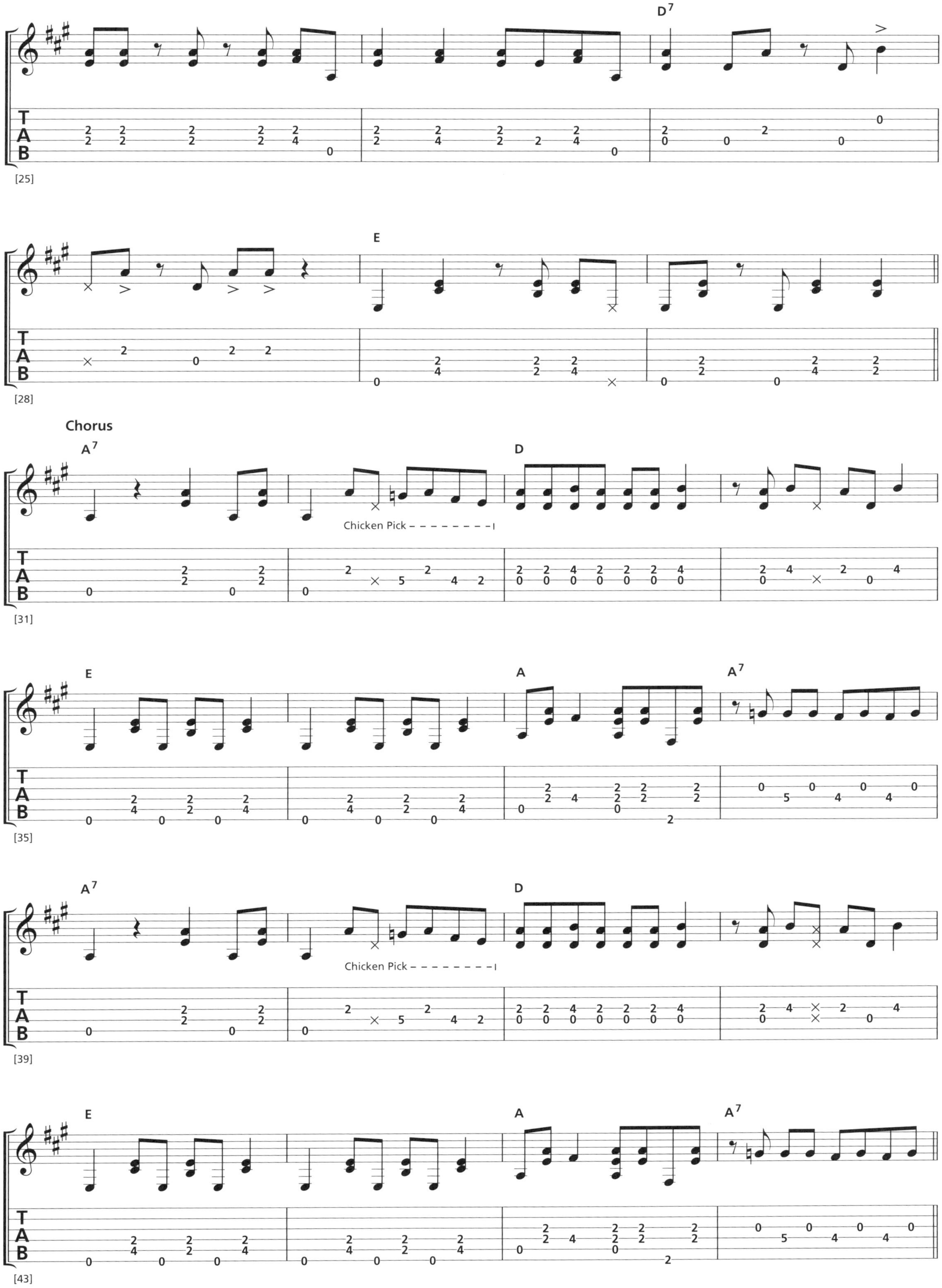
D7
[25]
E
[28]
Chorus
A7
Chicken Pick
D
[31]
E
A
A7
[35]
A7
Chicken Pick
D
[39]
E
A
A7
[43]

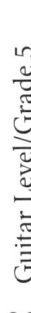

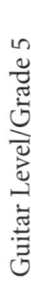

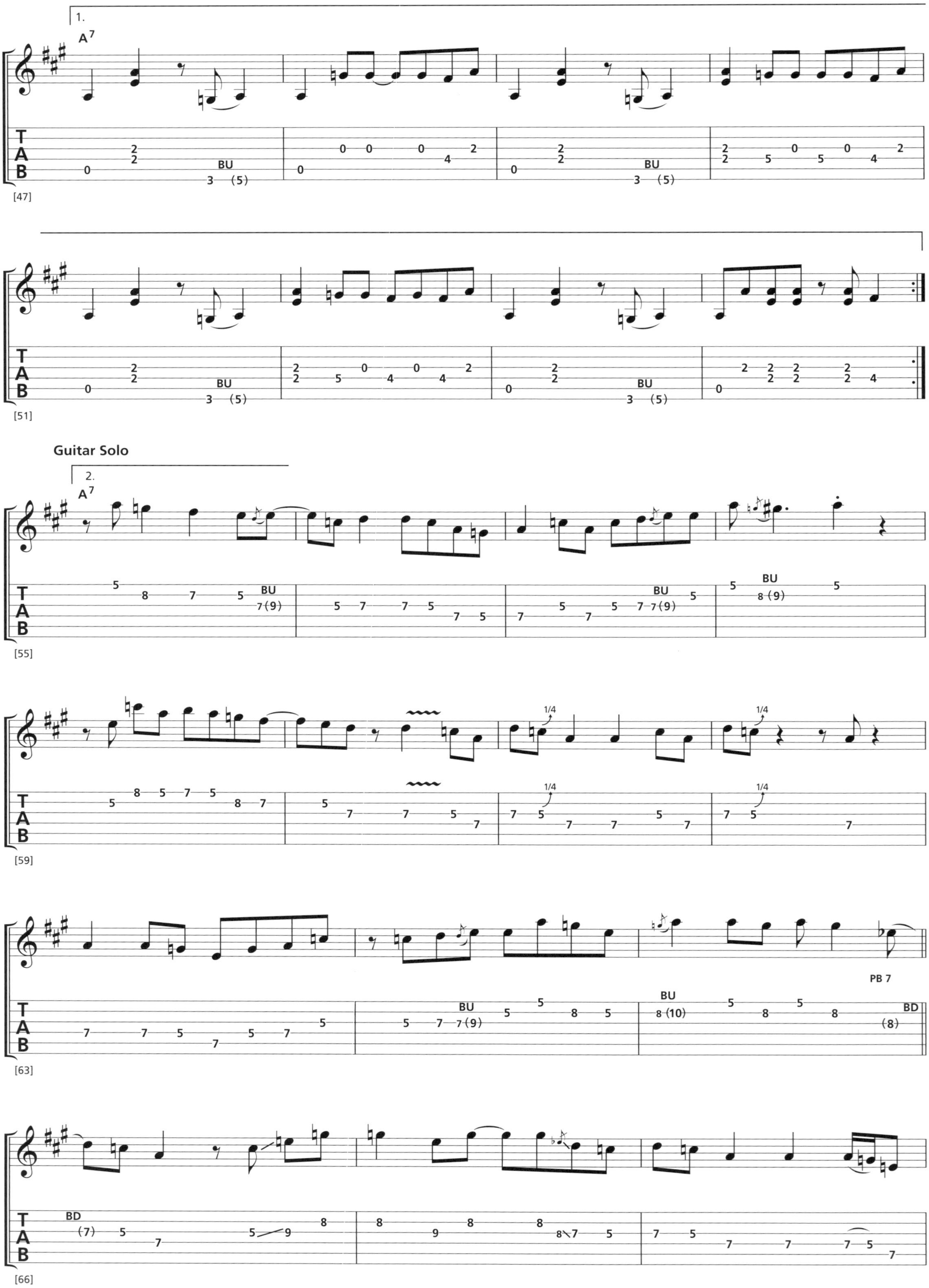

1.
A7
BU
[47]
[51]
Guitar Solo
2.
A7
BU
[55]
1/4
[59]
BU
PB 7
BD
[63]
BD
[66]

[69]
[72]
[75]
[78]
[81]
[84]
TAB
BU
BD
slow

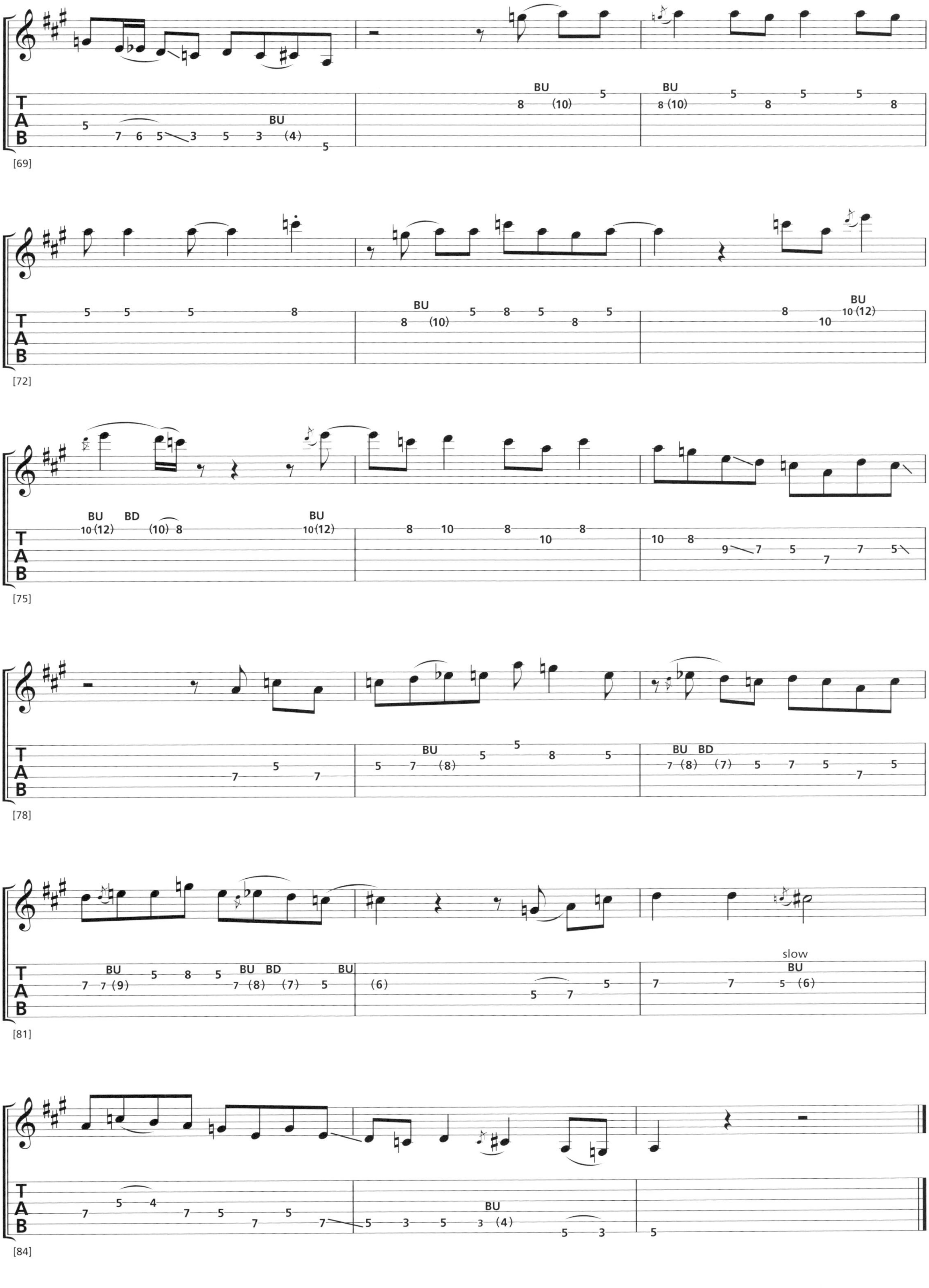

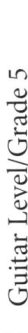

Walkthrough

Amp Settings

The sound should be full with a little rough 'edge', but not fully overdriven. It's a good idea to aim for a classic modern country sound rather than a heavy blues rock tone. If you had the choice of an amp model, 'American clean' would be a suitable choice – preferably a 50s type amp with a touch of compression, if available. On a three pickup single coil pickup type guitar, a suitable choice would be position 2.

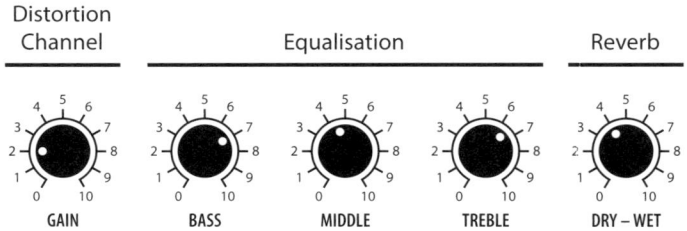

Intro Section (Measures 1–8)

The guitar part in the intro is classic country rock. You could be forgiven for thinking that Albert Lee had played on this session – and even though he didn't it's worth noting that Albert did play with Eric for a while. The first measure is a funky hybrid-picked groove.

Measure 2
This is classic country rock. The open strings and the use of the unison G (the 7th) and the F♯ (the 6th degree) are firmly within the country style.

Measure 3
The bend from low G up a whole tone is demanding if you're not use to this approach. Practise the bend slowly until you develop the required strength in your left hand. As always, sound a fretted destination note before trying to bend to the same pitch.

Verse and Chorus (Measures 17–54)

The groove is developed here. Note how the same idea is followed through the chord changes.

Measures 17–20
This is the template for the rest of the groove. Essentially the notes F♯ and G are used to spice up the basic A voicing.

Measure 27
The 6th degree is added over the D in this measure, to embellish the part.

Measure 29
Here the same technique is used on the low E voicing.

Guitar Solo Section (Measures 55–86)

This solo is deceptively well constructed. Eric Clapton's casual delivery masks some tasteful ideas over the chords.

Measure 55
Firstly, we have a run descending through the A mixolydian mode from the root.

Measure 56
Here Eric takes a bluesy but country-influenced approach by using the minor 3rd. It's worth noting that for most of this solo he uses the minor 3rd in preference to the major 3rd. Eric's bending in this solo is a by-product of his mastery of blues guitar forged during the 1960s.

Measure 59
This almost sounds like a jazz influenced line, due to slightly less common tensions – after the minor 3rd we have the 9th degree then the root and major 6th degree.

Measure 61–68
This section is more traditional, being based on the A minor pentatonic.

Measure 69
This is a more sophisticated idea. It appears as if it's going to run down the blues scale, however, in the second half of the measure the major 3rd of A (C♯) is approached from a semitone above then a semitone below. This approach is very popular in jazz.

Measures 73–76
Here Eric steps up a gear with some tasteful bends, more in keeping with his heritage as a leading blues rock player with John Mayall's Bluesbreakers and Cream. Eric's phrasing always has a certain class to it, and this is a perfect example of how deceptive his playing can be. The relaxed sound of this record obscures these incredible bends – the G to A and the D to E bends both have an incredible sound to them. Practise them slowly, and when you feel they are in tune start experimenting by adding vibrato to the bend. When you apply vibrato it's good to have a steady rhythmic pulse to the change in pitch.

AC/DC

SONG TITLE: HELL AIN'T A BAD PLACE TO BE
ALBUM: LET THERE BE ROCK
LABEL: ALBERT/ATLANTIC
GENRE: HARD ROCK / BLUES ROCK

WRITTEN BY: ANGUS YOUNG, MALCOLM YOUNG AND BON SCOTT
PRODUCED BY: HARRY VANDA AND GEORGE YOUNG

US CHART PEAK: 154

BACKGROUND INFO

'Hell Ain't A Bad Place To Be' is featured on AC/DC's fourth studio album *Let There Be Rock* released in July 1977. By then AC/DC had become a highly successful act in their native Australia and their popularity was increasing in the UK and Europe, primarily on the strength of their live shows. The band toured relentlessly and all previous records had been made in several studio sessions. Records were altered for international release and their fortunes in the US were mixed, with Atlantic Records refusing to release their third album *Dirty Deeds Done Dirt Cheap*, alleging the production was below par. With this in mind the band recorded *Let There Be Rock* in one go and the result captured their sound in a way their prior albums didn't. Many critics state that *Let There Be Rock* is the first true AC/DC album. During the recording of the solo for 'Whole Lotta Rosie' Angus Young's amp was smoking, it blew up, and in true rock and roll fashion they carried on and captured what became a legendary performance.

Bassist Cliff Williams joined the group after *Let There Be Rock* was released, replacing original bassist Mark Evans. In 1980 Brian Johnson replaced lead singer Bon Scott after the latter's sudden death. The band had released *Highway To Hell* and were on the verge of a commercial breakthrough. Upon Scott's death they considered disbanding but, encouraged by support from Scott's parents, they decided to the contrary and five months after recruiting Johnson they recorded *Back In Black*, dedicated to Scott's memory. The record is the second best-selling album in history. AC/DC became one of the biggest band's on earth and kept on touring relentlessly and releasing successful records.

In 2014 Malcolm Young retired, due to the early onset of dementia, and in 2016 Brian Johnson was advised to stop performing due to worsening hearing loss – he was replaced by Axl Rose from Guns N' Roses, who completed the remainder of their last tour.

AC/DC have sold over 200 million records and are hailed by many fans, critics and musicians as the greatest rock and roll band of all time. Malcolm Young passed away in November 2017, aged 64. He is acknowledged as one of the best rock and roll rhythm guitarists of all time.

Hell Ain't A Bad Place To Be

AC/DC
Words & Music by Angus Young,
Malcolm Young & Bon Scott

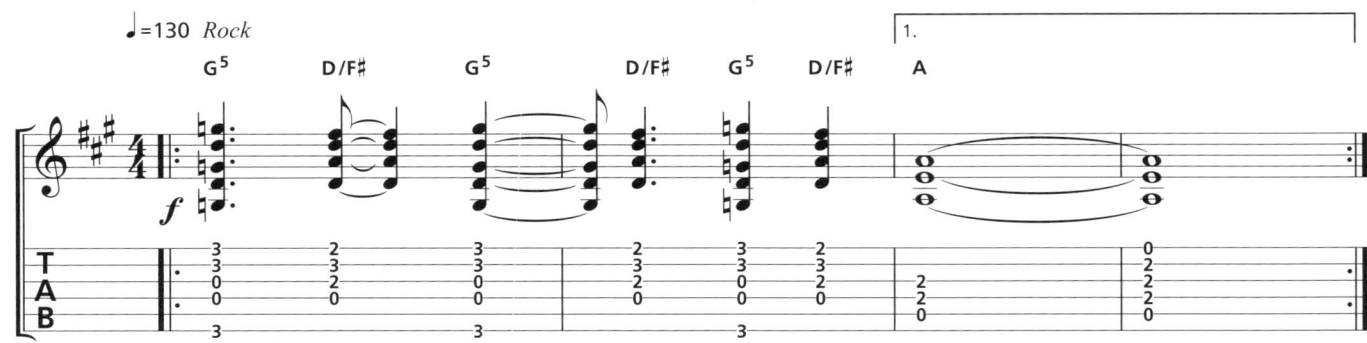

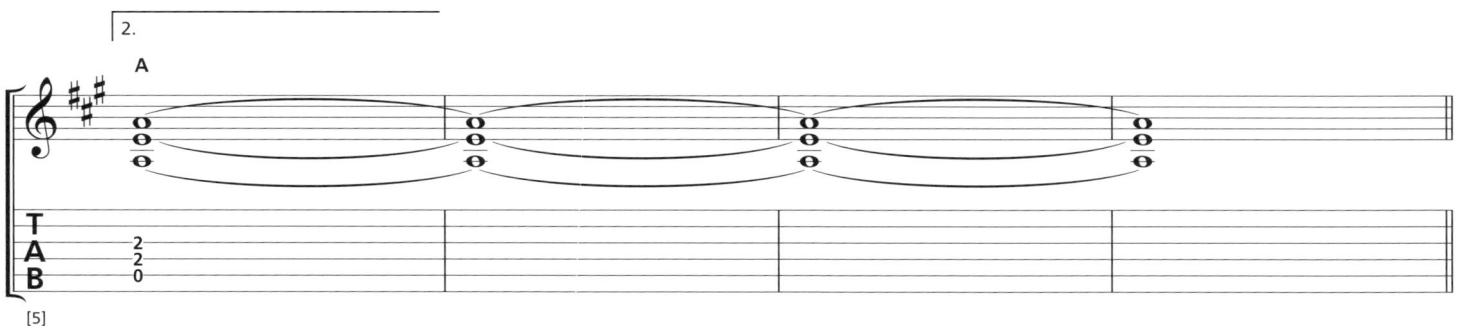

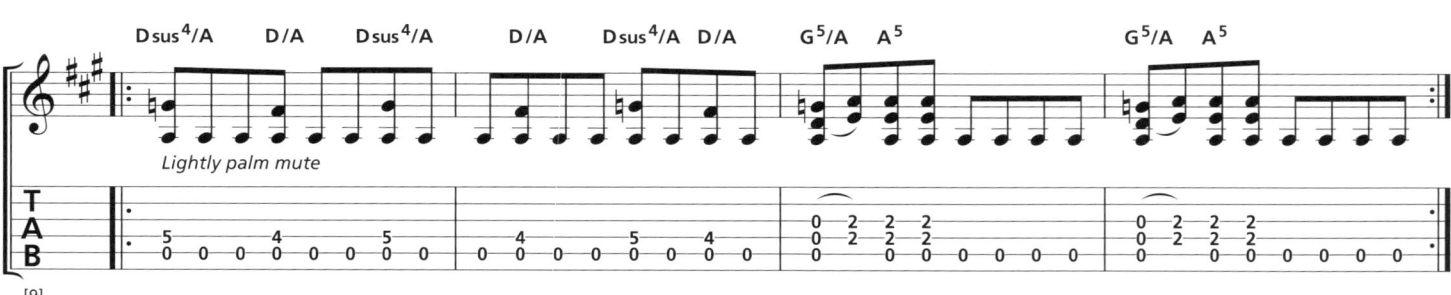

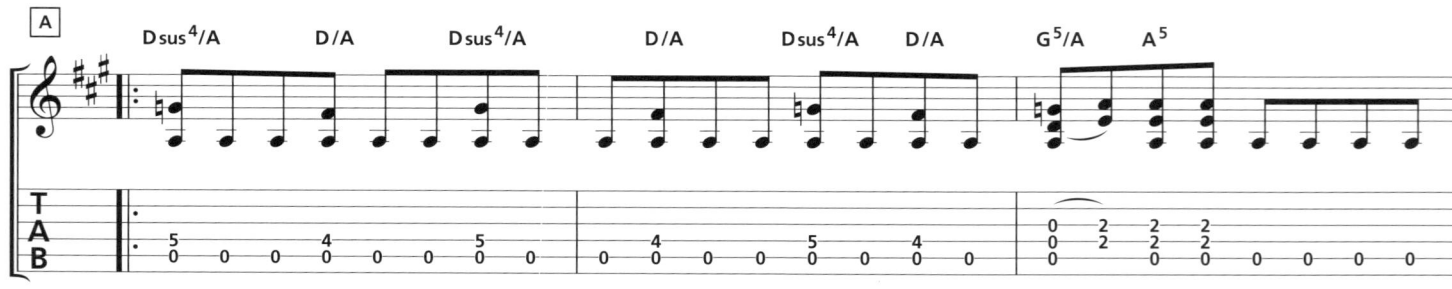

© Copyright 1977 J. Albert & Son Pty. Limited.
All Rights Reserved. International Copyright Secured.

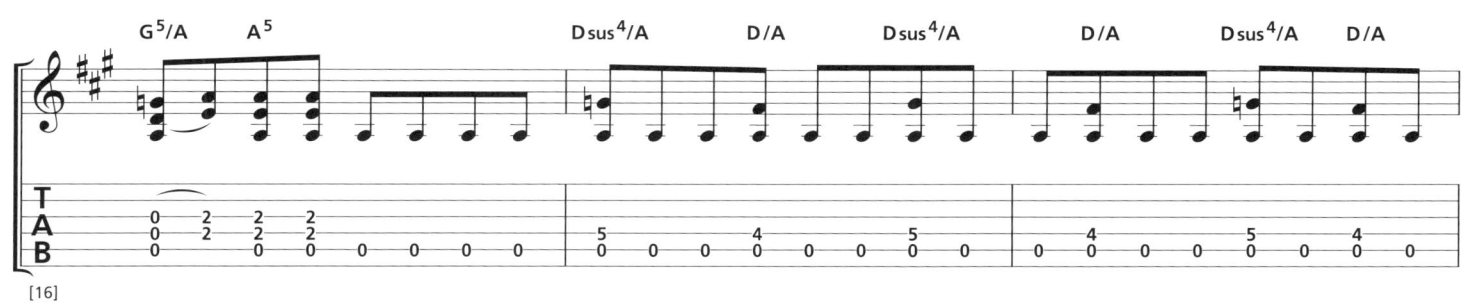
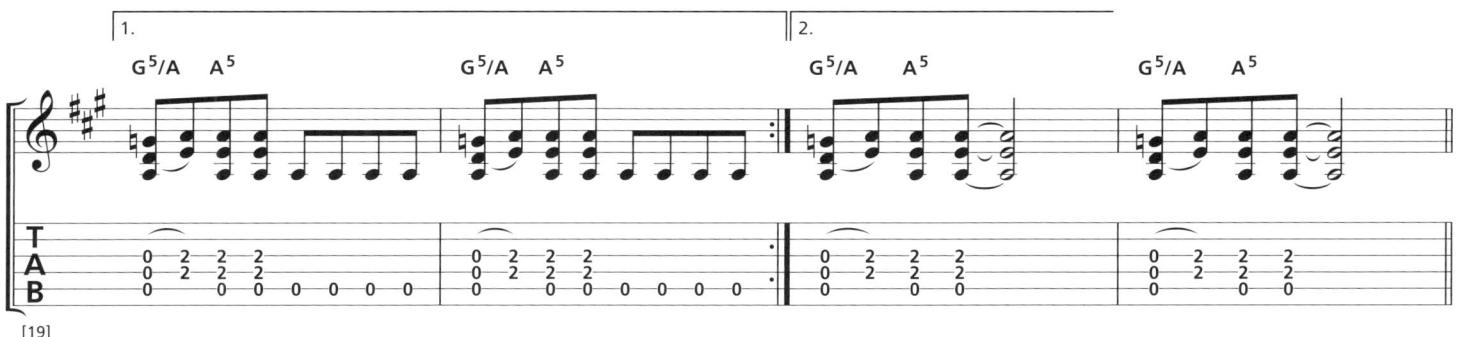
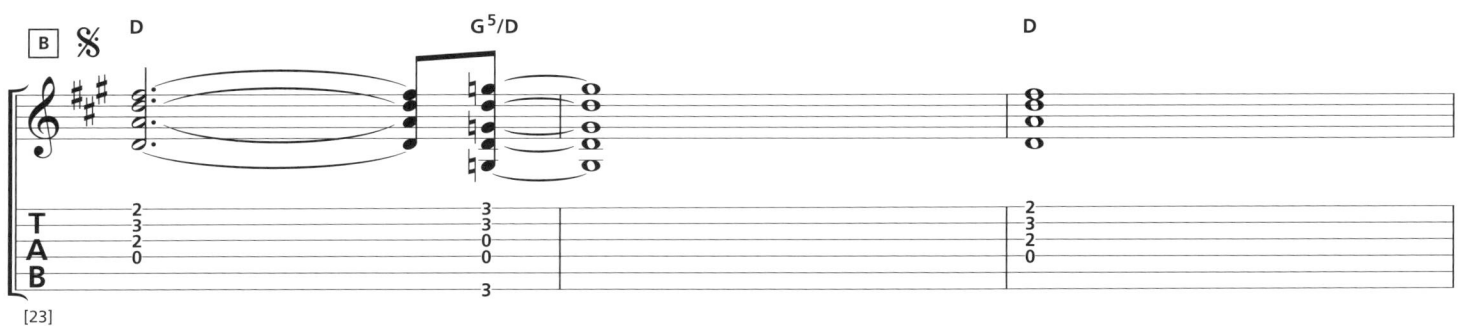
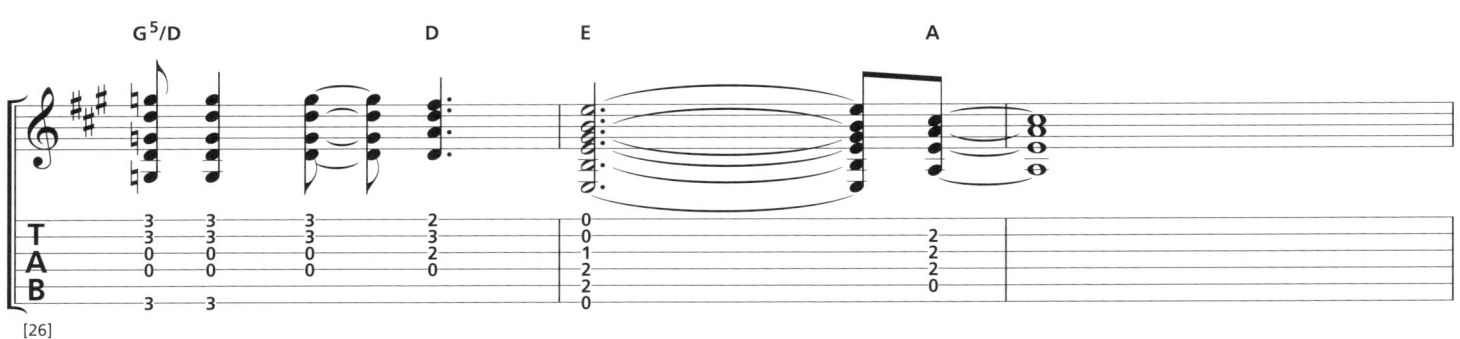
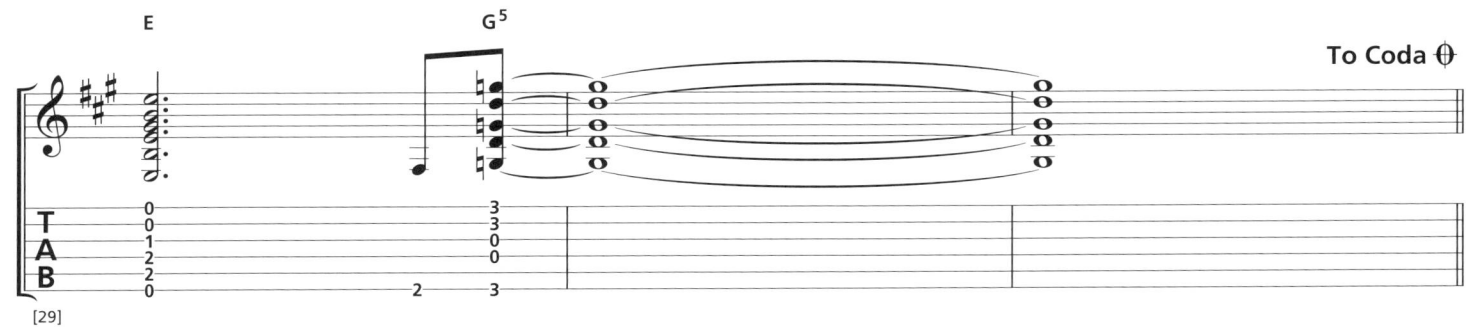

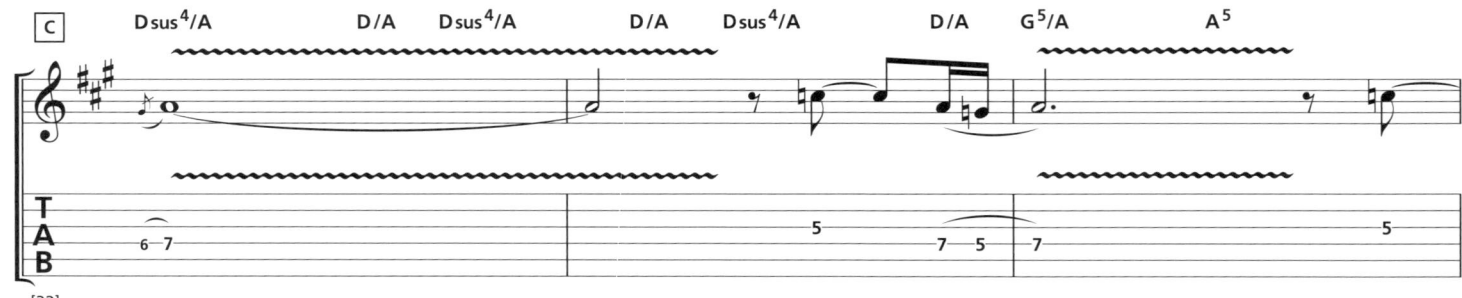
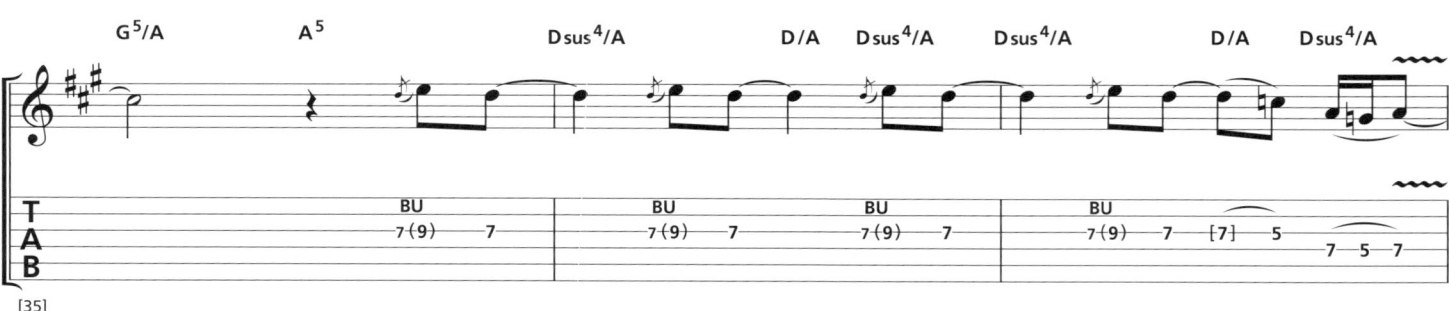
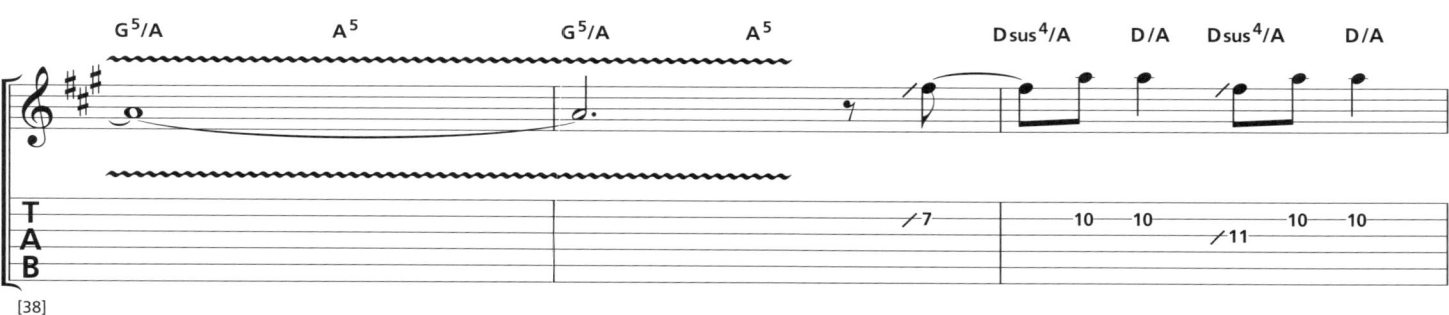
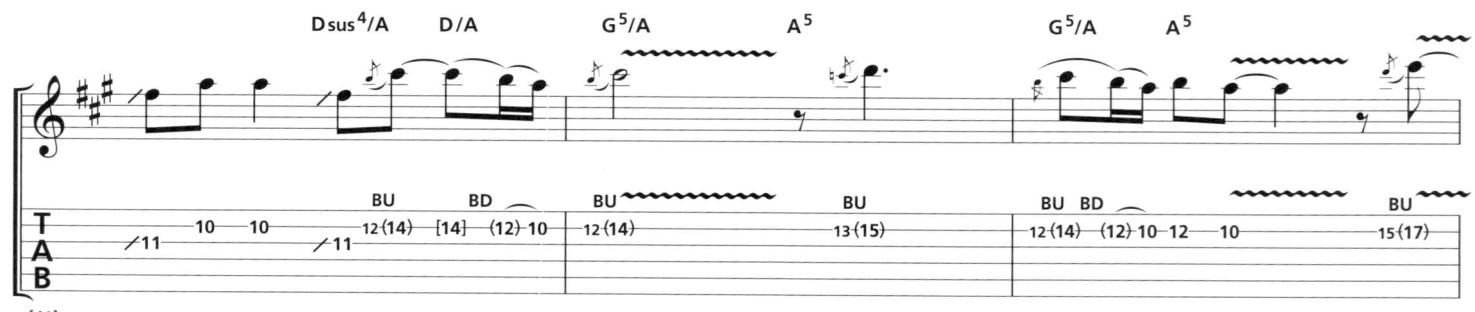

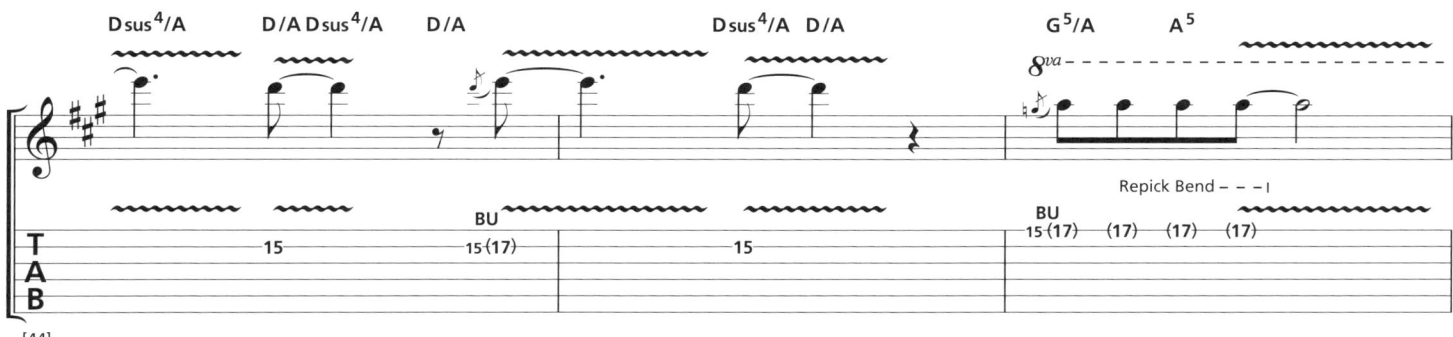
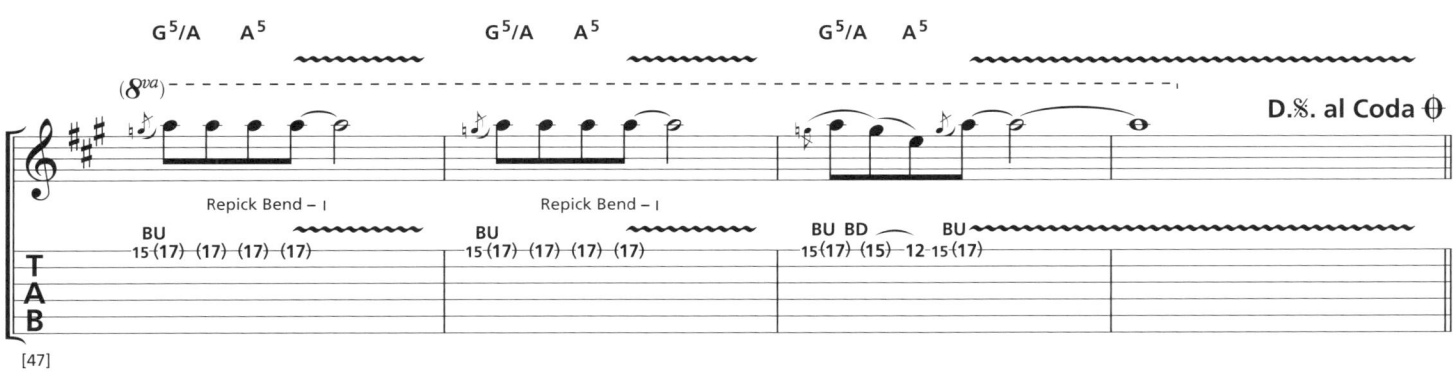
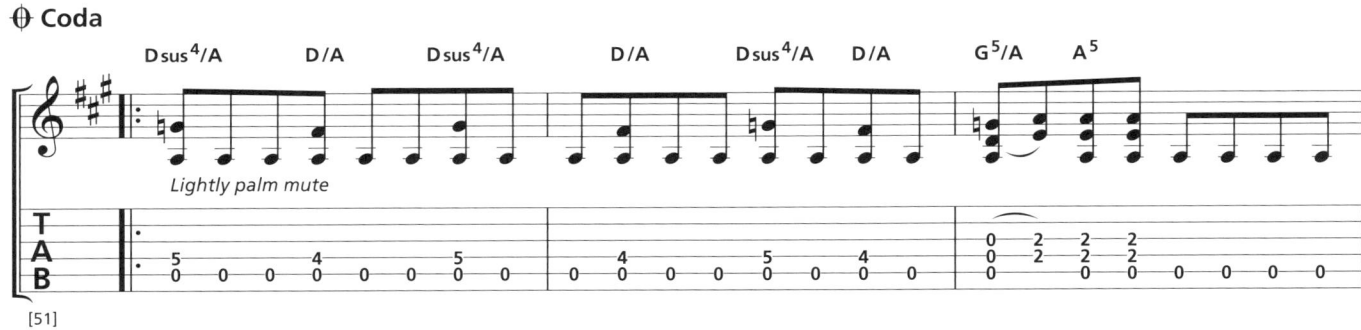
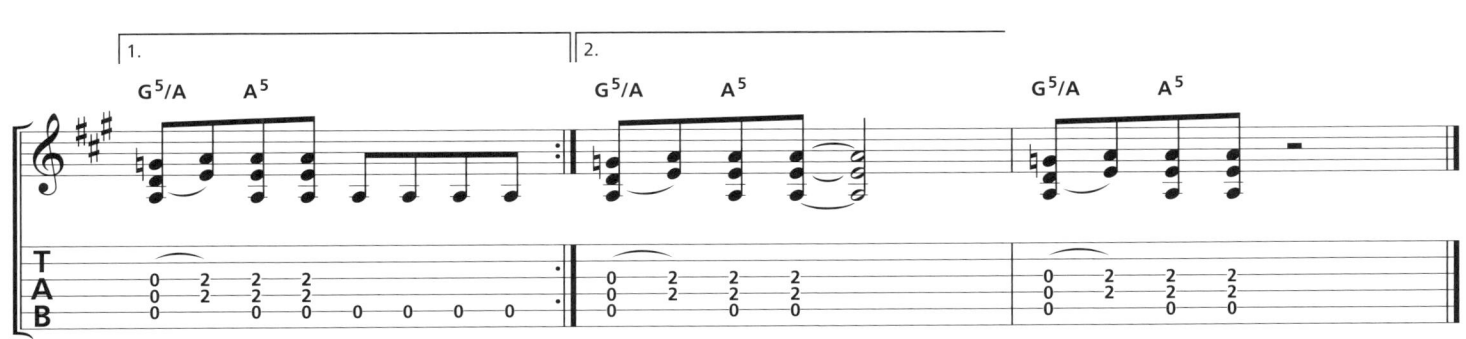

Walkthrough

Amp Settings

Malcolm and Angus Young used a very simple set up, with Angus playing a Gibson SG guitar and Malcolm a Gretsch, both into Marshall amplifiers. To achieve a similar sound a guitar fitted with hum-buckers will work well. Try experimenting with the levels of Bass, Middle and Treble and see what your ears like the sound of. Experiment with pickup selection and tone controls on the guitar and see what different tonal colours you like and feel suit the sound of the song the best.

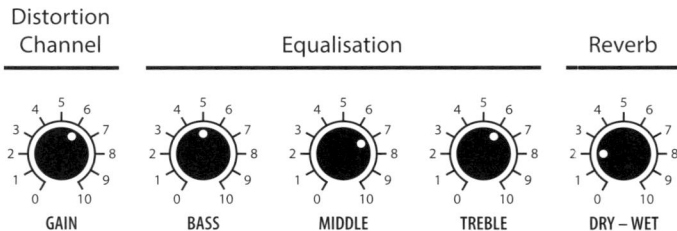

Intro

The intro begins with the guitar playing a G^5 ($\flat 7$) to D/F♯ (IV), before resolving to A^5 (I). Be careful not to play the B (major 3rd) on the A string on the G^5 chord.

A Section (Verse)

The main riff is a combination of Angus and Malcolm Young's guitar parts from the original version. The riff is based around the notes G to F♯ with a driving eighth rhythm played on the open A string, before hammering on to an A^5 from the open A, D, and G strings (G/A).

B Section (Pre – chorus)

In the B section the guitar plays a rhythmic figure moving between a D (IV) to G^5 ($\flat$VII) in measures 23–26, whilst the bass guitar plays eighth notes on a static D. At measure 27 the guitar plays E (V) to A^5 (I) before landing on the G^5 ($\flat$vii) for the last two measures, leading into section C.

C Section (solo)

The solo is based around major and minor pentatonic licks in the key of A. The solo starts with phrases played in the first position of the A minor pentatonic from measures 32 to 37. From measure shifts to the third position of the major pentatonic until measure 44 where the guitar plays long held notes from the 4th to the 5th of the scale, then from measure 46 until the end, $\flat 7$ to the root. Work on getting a consistent vibrato on these long bends. At the end of the solo take the *D.S.* back to pre-chorus and continue until measure 31 (*To Coda* sign) then jump to measure 51.

Coda section

The song returns to the main riff to end the song.

If you are struggling with any parts in the song try isolating the measures that you want to focus on and practice them in isolation without the backing track. It may also help to play along with just a metronome to help focus on the areas that you feel may need attention. Try keeping time yourself by tapping your foot or nodding your head in time with the music. This will help develop your 'inner clock'.

Geek

SONG TITLE: GEEK
GENRE: POP PUNK
TEMPO: 137 BPM
KEY: E MAJOR

TECH FEATURES: PALM MUTING
TRIPLET RHYTHMS
STRING SKIPPING

COMPOSER: JAMES UINGS

PERSONNEL: STUART RYAN (GTR)
DAVE MARKS (BASS)
NOAM LEDERMAN (DRUMS)

OVERVIEW

'Geek' is a pop punk piece in the style of Green Day, The Offspring and Billy Talent that features, among other techniques, palm-muting, powerchords, hammer-ons and pull-offs.

STYLE FOCUS

From a guitarist's perspective, punk rock in its purest form is a simple style of music. In terms of rhythm playing and harmony, most punk guitar is limited to powerchords. Solos are rare. However, bands like Green Day, The Offspring, Billy Talent and The Clash before them have been known to incorporate techniques, time signatures and chord patterns from outside the usual punk boundaries.

THE BIGGER PICTURE

The Clash were one of the first punk groups to absorb influences from other genres; their later albums owed as much to rockabilly and reggae as they did the Ramones. Although they were criticised by some, The Clash set an example that was to result in later punk groups adopting a more diverse approach to the development of their sounds.

Green Day, another band that set out in a narrow punk field, signed to a major record label and absorbed techniques and songwriting tricks alien to their genre. This may have seemed strange from frontman Billie Joe Armstrong, whose influences were ostensibly his local punk scene and the groups Hüsker Dü and The Replacements. However, he grew up singing jazz at home with his drummer father and has professed a love of The Who and Cheap Trick.

Green Day's contemporaries The Offspring always had a metal edge to their sound and became more open to outside influences as their career progressed. *Americana*, their 1998 album, jumped from new wave to hip hop to rocksteady to mariachi. In the 2000s, Billy Talent's Ian D'Sa introduced a pick and fingers technique inspired by Mark Knopfler of Dire Straits and chord work similar to that of his hero Andy Summers of The Police.

RECOMMENDED LISTENING

Green Day's operatic *American Idiot* (2004) is a rarity among punk rock albums, yet similar to The Who's *Tommy* (1969). The Offspring's *Americana* is their most diverse album to date, while *Billy Talent II* (2006) is a showcase for D'Sa's inventive playing.

Geek

James Uings

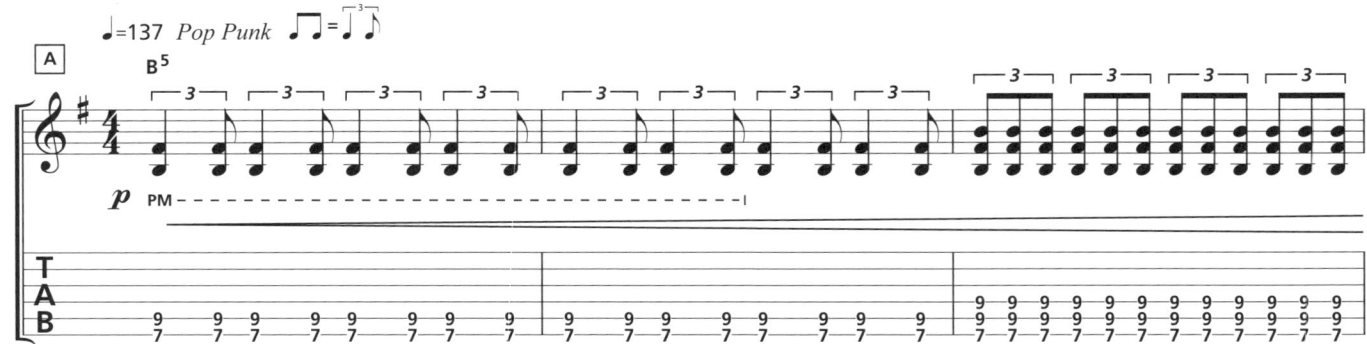
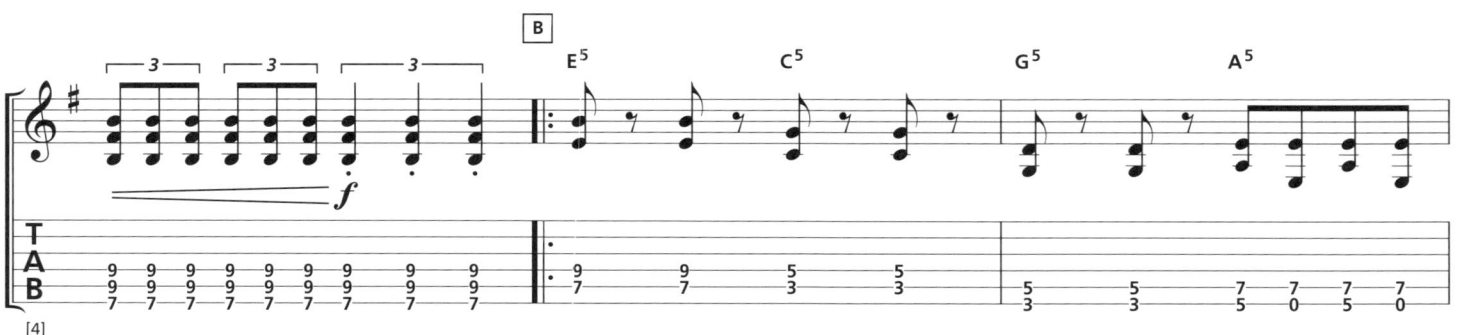

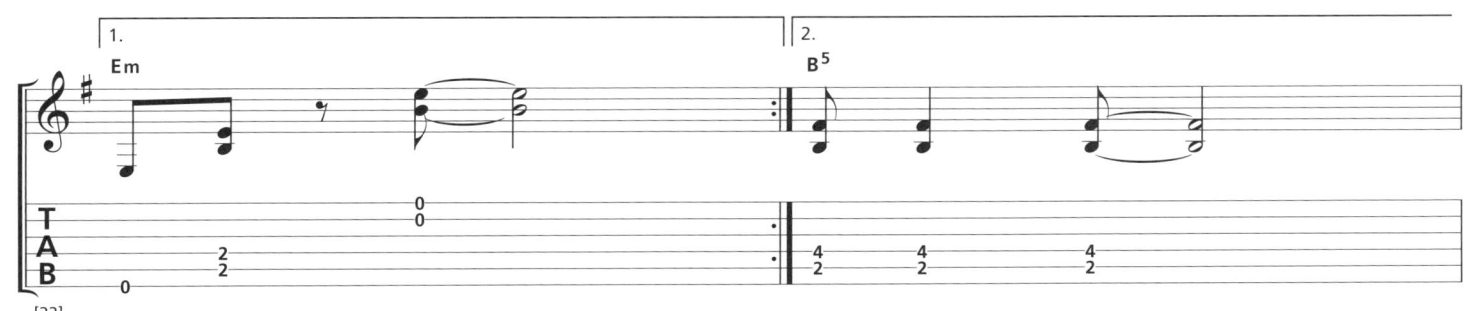

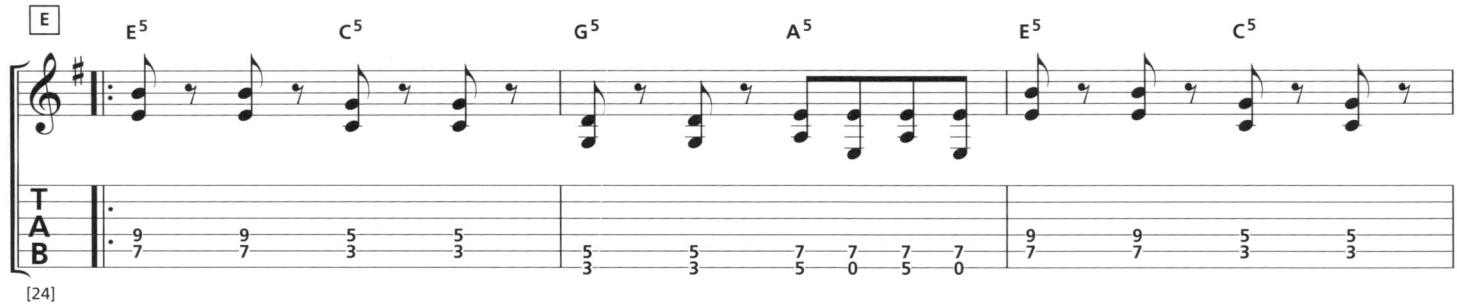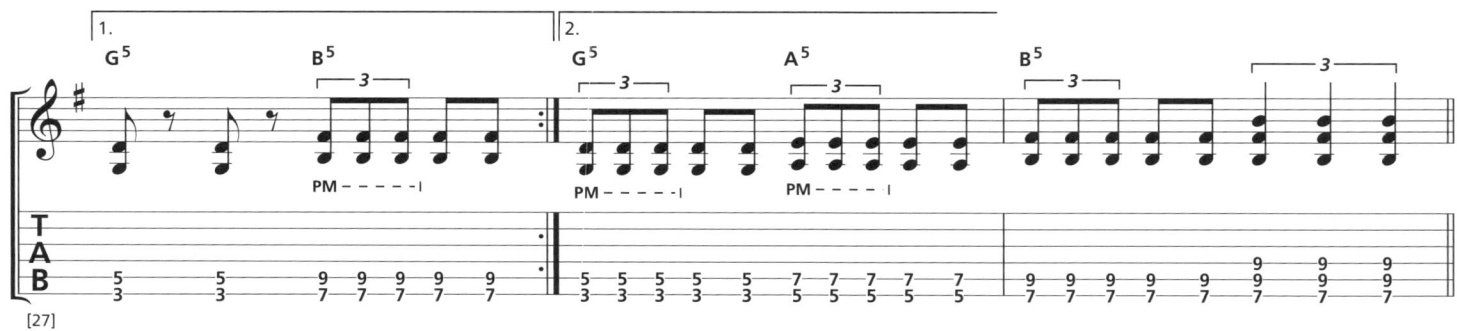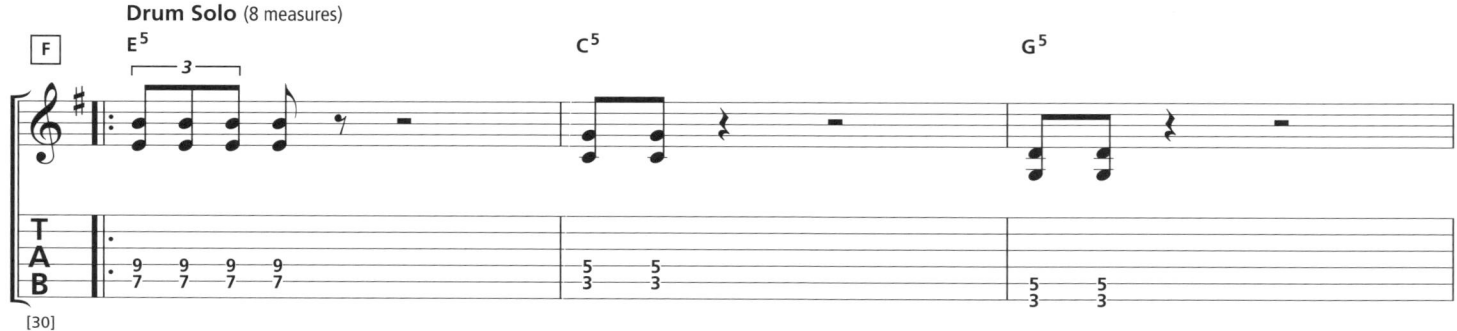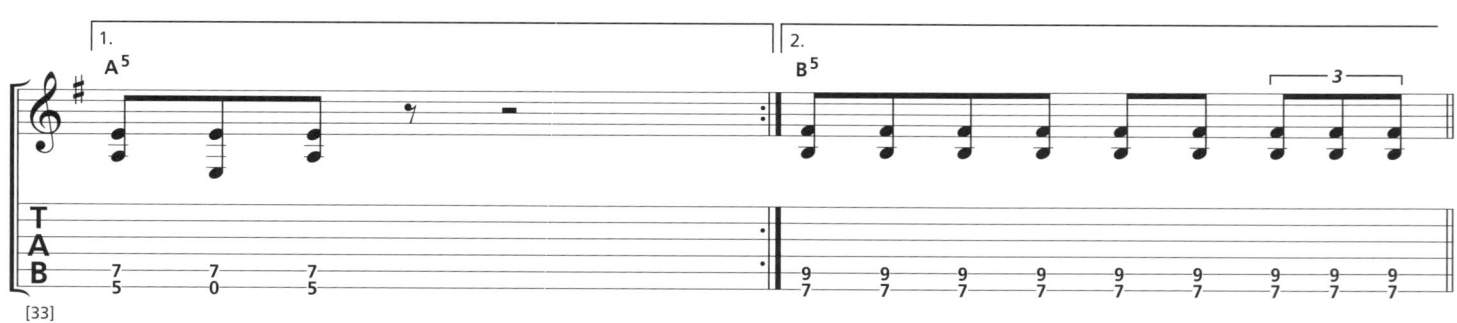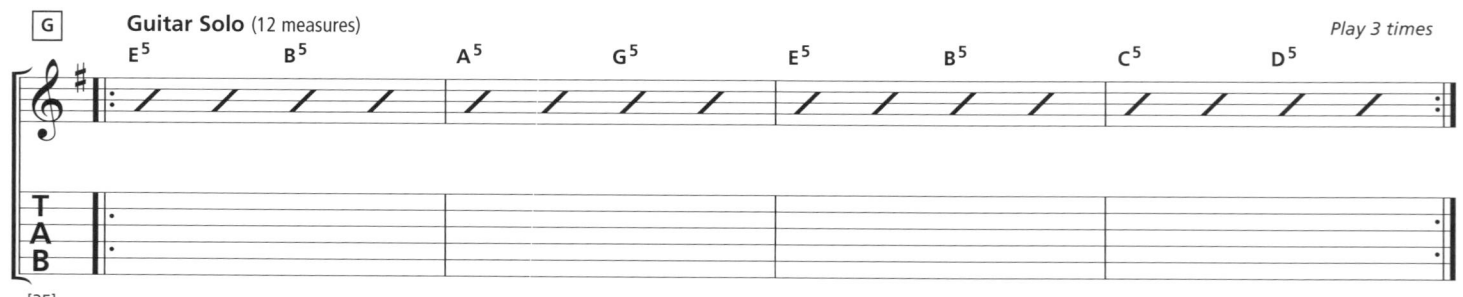

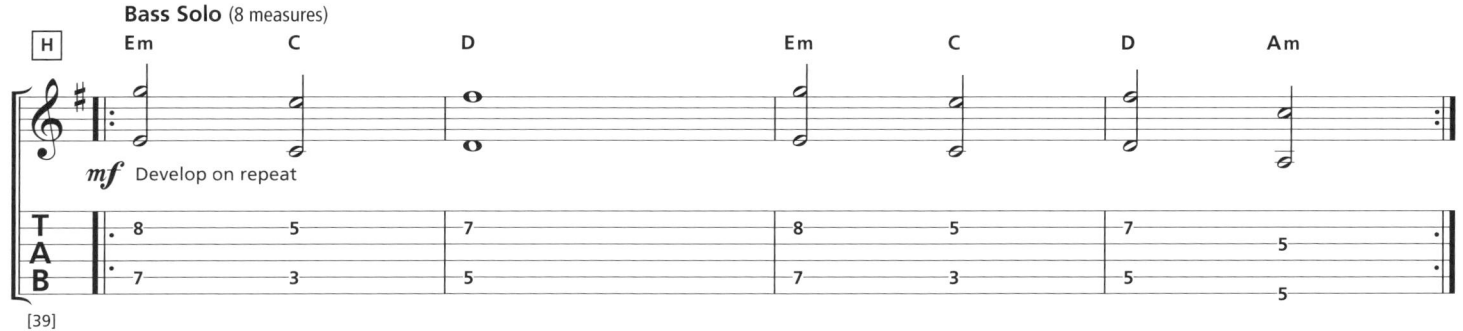
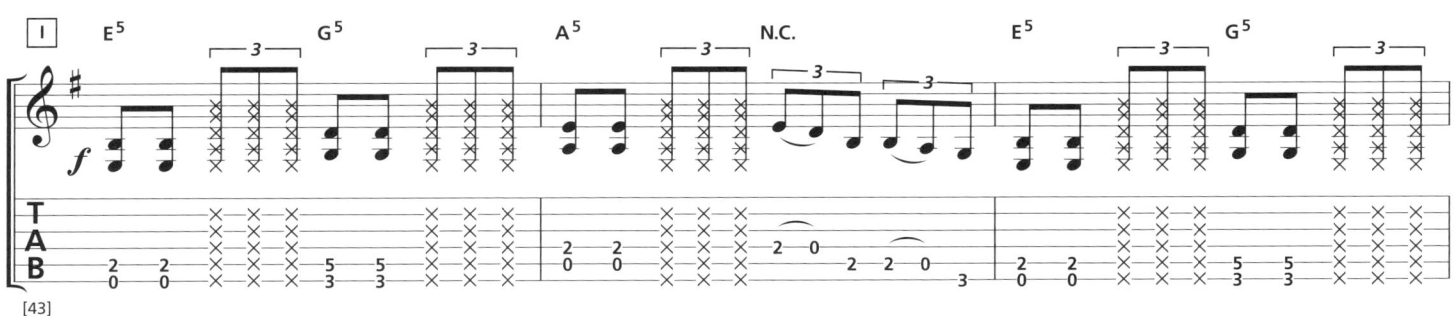
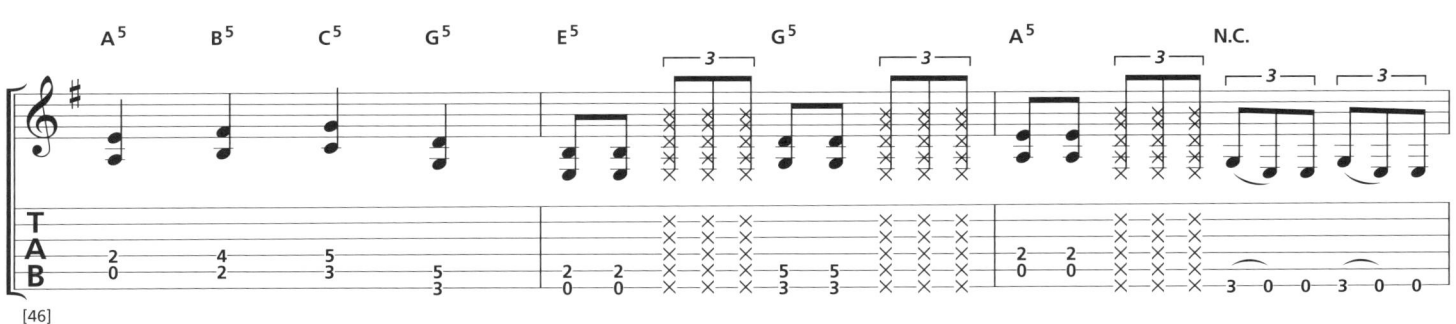
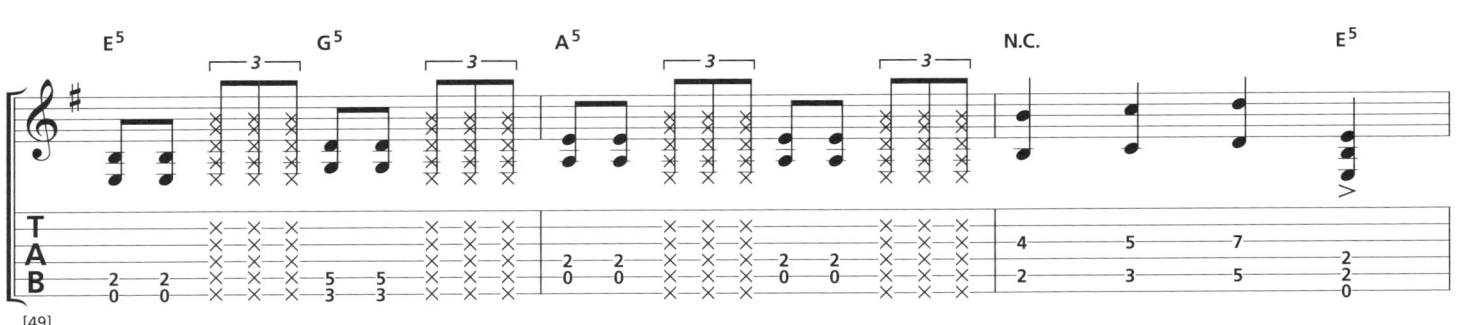

Walkthrough

Amp Settings

A modern high-gain distortion with the gain set relatively high will give you the saturated distortion you are looking for. Rock, punk and metal guitar tones use a lot less reverb than other styles so be careful with the amount you add or it will reduce the effectiveness of the tight, snappy parts.

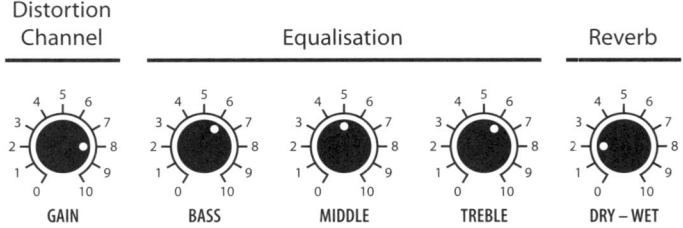

A Section (Measures 1–4)
This section is a three-and-a-half measure crescendo on a single chord that builds from a swung rhythm to triplets before ending on a quarter-note triplet.

Measures 1–54 | Triplet picking
The triplet rhythm is used throughout 'Geek', and the odd number of notes can make picking triplets a challenge. At this high tempo they will have to be played using alternate picking/strumming, so some beats will start with an upstroke that may feel unusual to you at first (Fig. 1).

B Section (Measures 5–10)
This powerchord riff moves quickly around the fretboard.

Measures 5–10 | Moving powerchords
As you move between the powerchords, lock your fingers in position and shift your whole hand rather than individual fingers to make your changes faster and more efficient.

C Section (Measures 11–18)
This is a single-note melody that uses palm-mutes, octaves and slides. It contains a lot of fretboard movement, so maintain a structured approach to your fingerings.

Measures 11–15 | Picking accuracy
These quick string skips must be executed accurately. Slow the phrase down to ensure you strike each note cleanly without making contact with the other strings.

D & E Sections (Measures 19–29)
The D section is another riff based on powerchords. Aside from chordal stabs, some chords are arpeggiated while being palm-muted. The E section is a reprise of the B section.

Measure 21 | Wide stretches
The movement of the G to the F♯ in this measure features a challenging stretch. Practise the same shape higher up the fretboard and move down a fret at a time until you are comfortable with the written part (Fig. 2).

F, G & H Sections (Measures 30–42)
These three sections are the drum, guitar and bass solos. The guitar plays chords at the beginning of each measure in the drum solo. The guitar solo enables you to create your own solo; vary the written part on the repeat in the bass solo.

Measures 35–38 | Melodic solos
Punk solos rarely use blues based pentatonic ideas. A more melodic approach (which could still use the minor pentatonic) may make your solo stylistically appropriate.

I Section (Measures 43–54)
These powerchords alternate with aggressively strummed muted strings, octaves and single note runs.

Measures 43–50 | Muting strings
To get the aggressive sound, place your picking hand lightly across the string and strum hard in the specified rhythm.

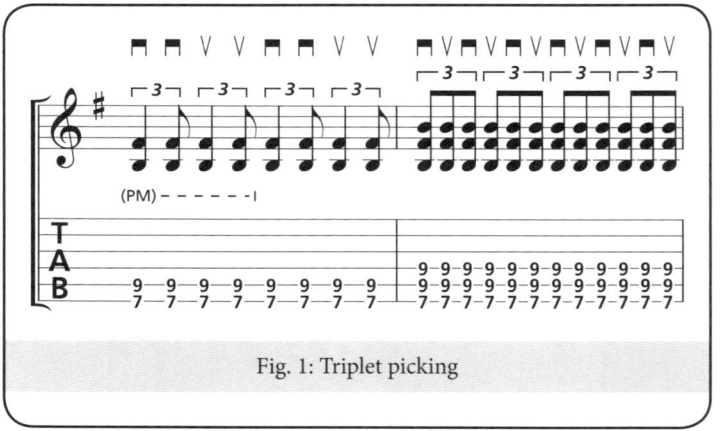

Fig. 1: Triplet picking

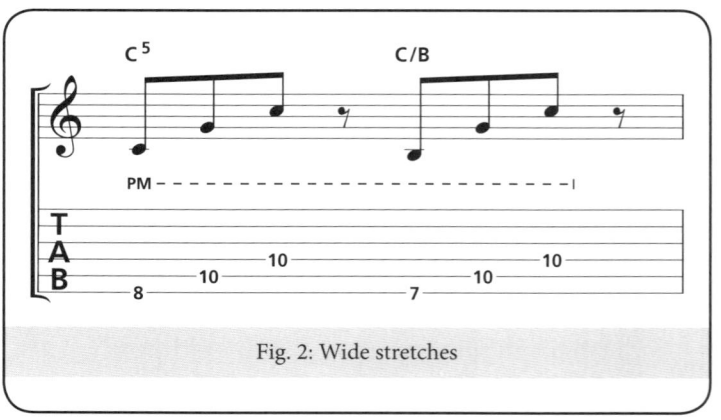

Fig. 2: Wide stretches

Rollin'

SONG TITLE: ROLLIN'
GENRE: BLUES ROCK
TEMPO: 107 BPM
KEY: B MINOR/D MAJOR

TECH FEATURES: DOUBLE-STOP RIFFS
STRING BENDS
SYNCOPATED RIFFS

COMPOSERS: STUART RYAN, HENRY THOMAS
& NOAM LEDERMAN

PERSONNEL: STUART RYAN (GTR)
HENRY THOMAS (BASS)
NOAM LEDERMAN (DRUMS)
ROSS STANLEY (KEYS)

OVERVIEW

'Rollin'' is a composition created in the style of American pop and blues rock singer-songwriter and guitarist John Mayer. This piece features rhythmic ideas built around double-stops, triads and arpeggiated chords, plus a melodic lead guitar part that is composed rather than improvised.

Mayer often works within the trio format of guitar, bass and drums, so when you learn 'Rollin'' be careful to listen out for the interplay between each of the instruments on the track.

STYLE FOCUS

Blues rock guitar typically features a power trio of guitar, bass and drums, possibly augmented by a Hammond organ or keys player. This style of music originated in the 1960s, when bands such as Cream and The Jimi Hendrix Experience fused traditional blues styles with the volume and tones of the rock guitar styles emerging at the time. Prodigious guitar talent Stevie Ray Vaughan developed this style of playing in the 1980s with a strong lean towards the blues, and Mayer fuses these particular influences with commercial sensibilities that have lead to a clutch of hit albums.

THE BIGGER PICTURE

Mayer draws influence from many guitarists, especially Hendrix and Vaughan. Blues remains at the heart of what he plays, especially when he solos. His guitar parts are always creative and laden with hooks, displaying his Hendrix and SRV influences. He is a guitarist of many colours. He's at home with complex fingerpicked acoustic guitar parts, roaring electric blues solos, and funk inspired rhythm playing. His success has enabled him to display several different musical guises from stripped back acoustic performer to leader of a blues power trio.

RECOMMENDED LISTENING

Since the early 2000s, Mayer has released several albums in a variety of musical settings. His major label debut, *Room For Squares* (2001), showcases his more pop oriented songwriting. You may also wish to check out its precursor, the all acoustic EP *Inside Wants Out* (1999). On *Continuum* (2006) he shines in the guitar, bass and drums format with session supremos Steve Jordan (drums) and Pino Palladino (bass). The same trio recorded the live blues oriented album *Try!* (2005), while *Where The Light Is: John Mayer Live In Los Angeles* (2008) features him in solo, trio and full band formats.

Rollin'

Stuart Ryan, Henry Thomas & Noam Lederman

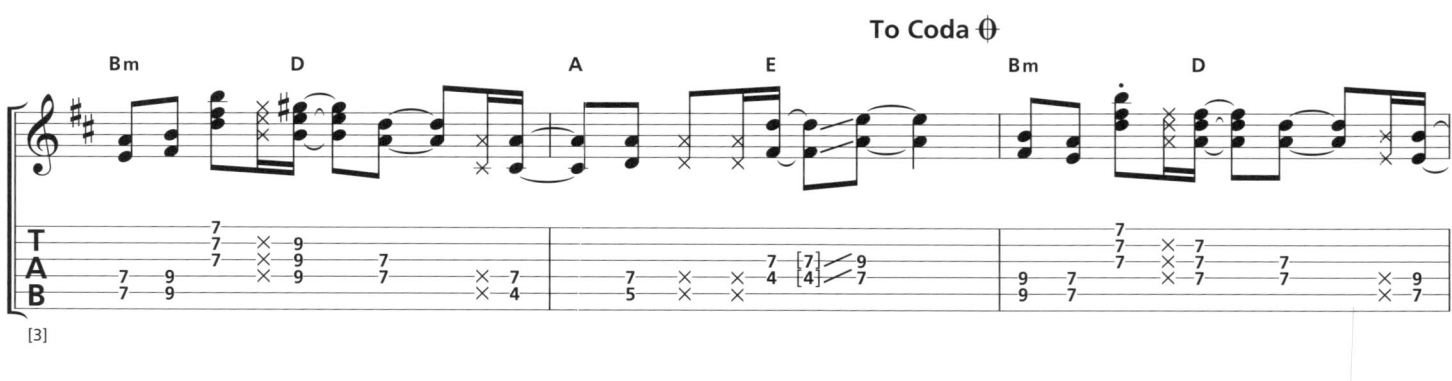
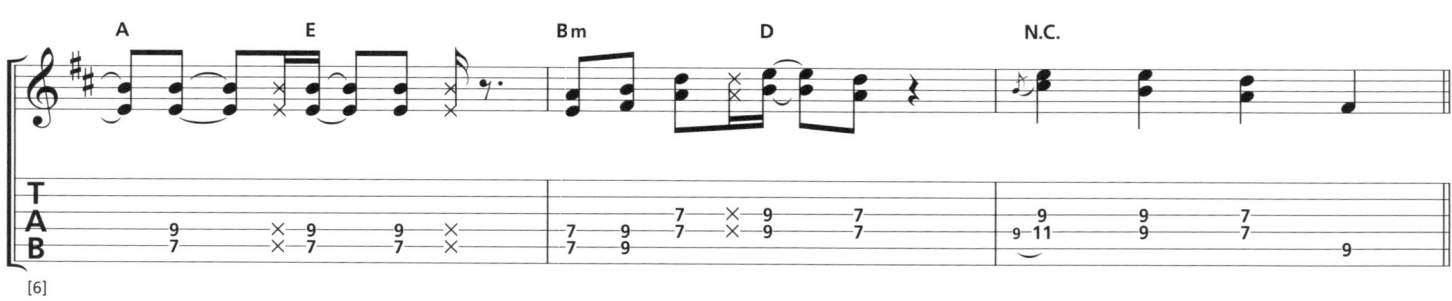

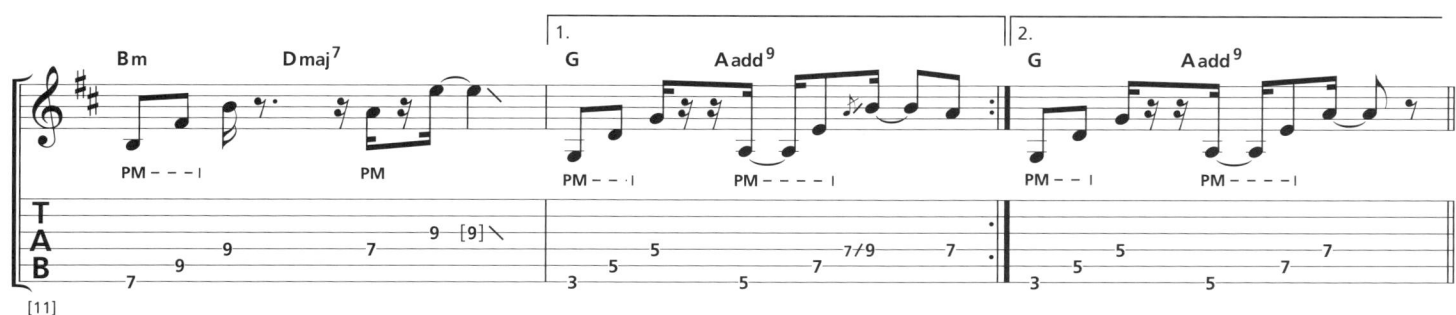
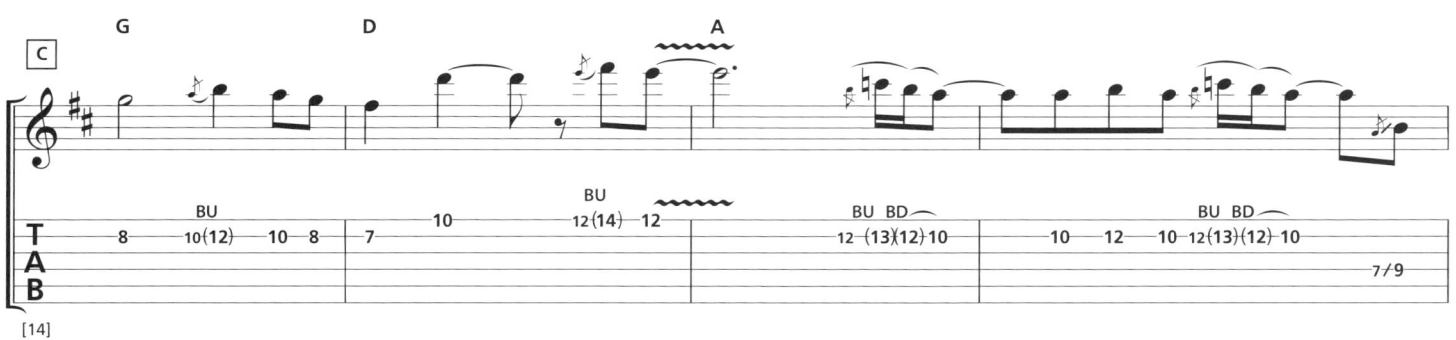
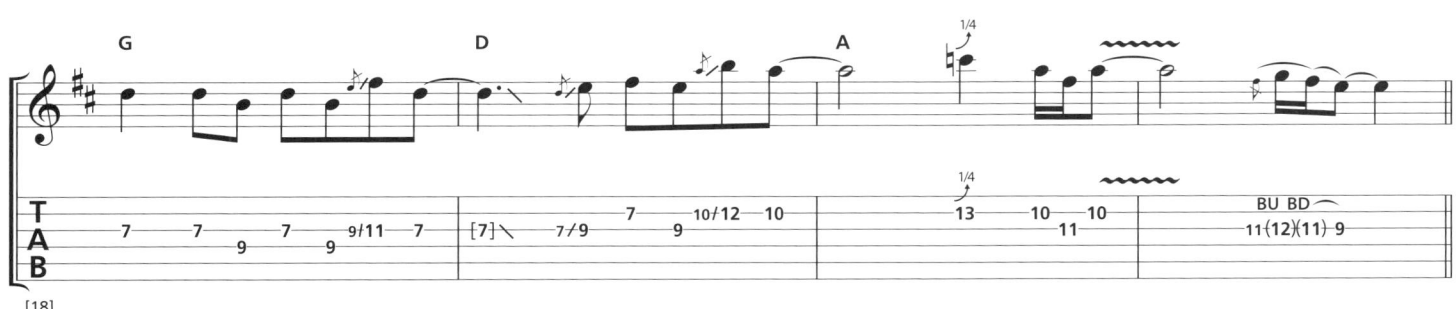

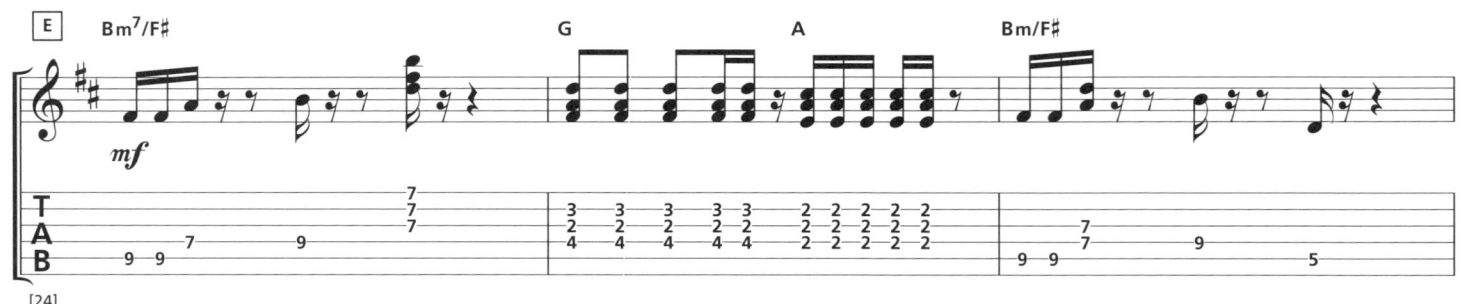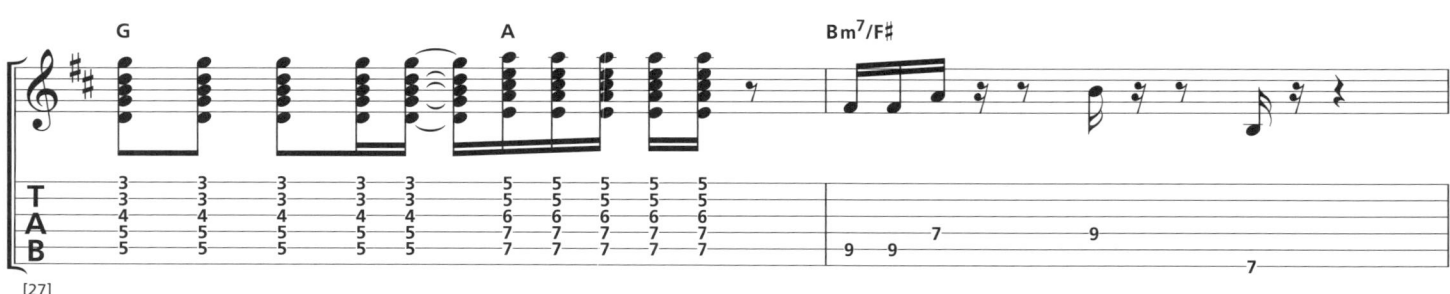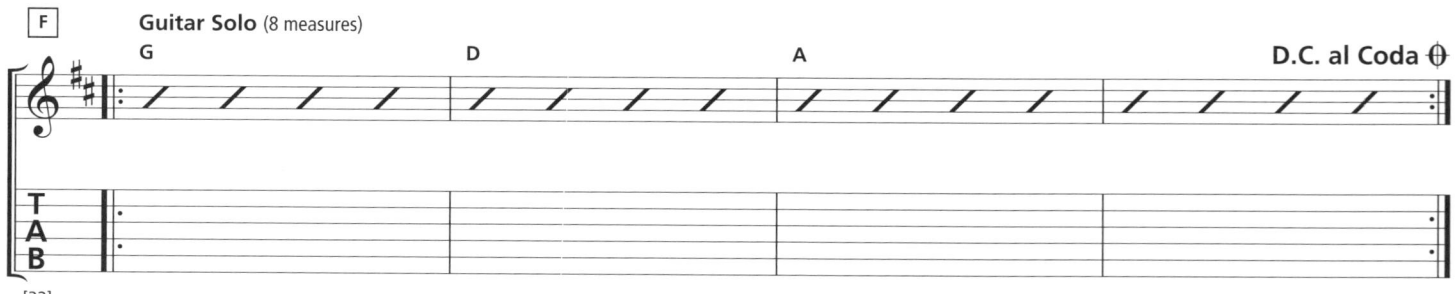

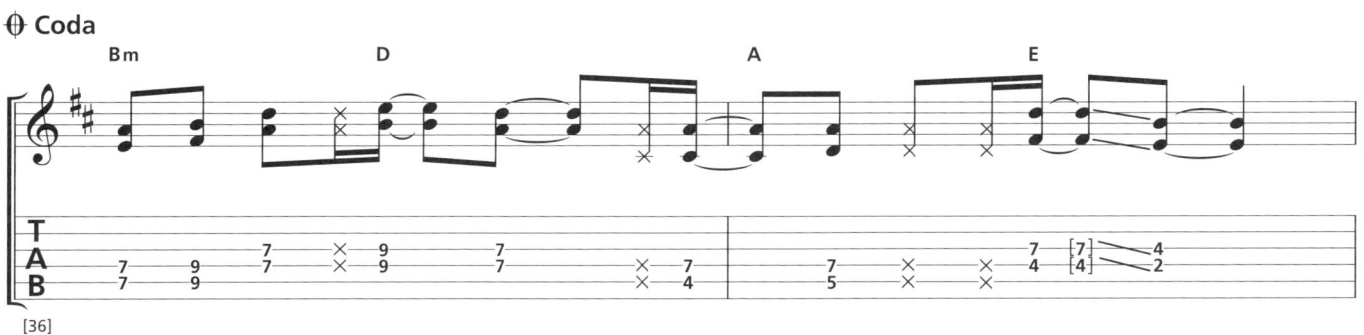
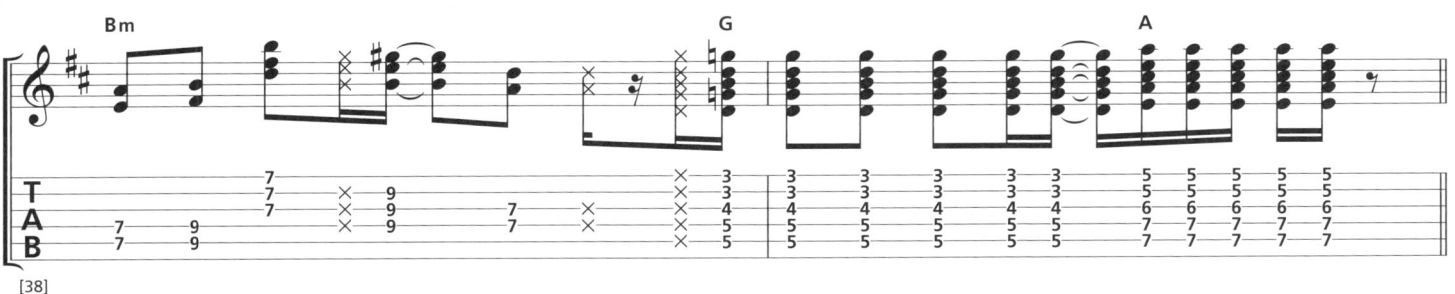
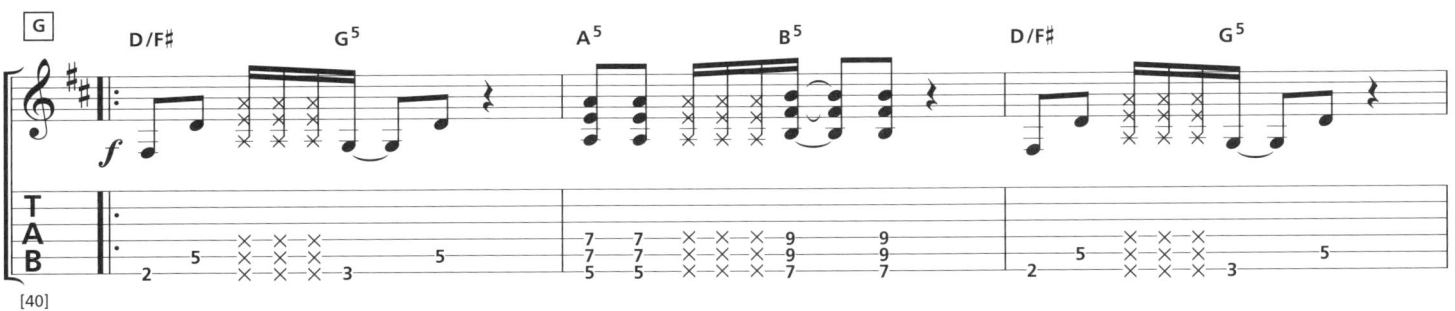

Walkthrough

Amp settings
Although an overdriven sound is suggested below, a clean tone will work just as well. If you opt for a distorted tone, set the gain to medium because the sound should only break up when you are playing your hardest.

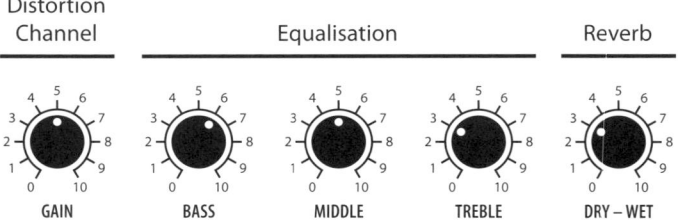

A Section (Measures 1–8)
The A section comprises a syncopated riff that plays double-stops and three-note chords. Although these could be interpreted as complex chord extensions (Bm^{11}, etc.), the chord symbols reflect the overall harmony of the piece.

Measures 1–45 | *Sixteenth-note syncopations*
There are many 16th-note syncopated rhythms throughout 'Rollin'', many of which will be easier to learn by ear than the notation might suggest. If you find that any rhythms are a particular problem, break down the measure into beats first and then 16th notes. Work slowly through the measure (Fig. 1).

B & C Sections (Measures 9–21)
The B section consists of low chord voicings played in a syncopated rhythm. The C section is a notated guitar solo that contains many key techniques found in blues rock.

Measures 16–21 | *Semitone bends*
Semitone bends are often overbent by inexperienced players who are used to the whole tone bends found in pentatonic solos. Playing the target note (the note in brackets) before you attempt the bend will help with the accuracy, as the target note is fresh in your memory.

D Section (Measures 22–23)
This section is the bass solo. The two measures are played four times. After the first time through you should develop the part using your own variations.

Measures 22–23 | *Developing a part*
When you develop a part, you should make sure you are faithful to the original that is notated while still taking the section somewhere new. Common ways to develop a part are to vary the rhythm, picking patterns or use different chord voicings.

These are, of course, only suggestions and you should play the part as you feel works best.

E Section (Measures 24–31)
This section alternates between a measure of syncopated riffing and chords played using 16th-note rhythms.

Measures 25–31 | *Ghost strums*
Keeping your hand in a constant strumming motion between chord hits will make the rhythm parts more fluent. When you don't want to strike the strings, move your pick a small amount away. These are called ghost strums (Fig. 2).

F & G Sections (Measures 32–45)
The F section is an improvised guitar solo while the G section is a low-string riff that combines single notes, powerchords and muted strings.

Measures 32–35 | *Guitar solo*
Although the first chord of the solo progression is a G, the key is firmly rooted in D major. Both the D major pentatonic and D major scales are ideal for soloing. It's a good idea to be aware of the notes in each of the progression's chords and their location within your chosen scale. This knowledge will enable you to resolve your licks and phrases on chord tones, giving them a sense of resolution.

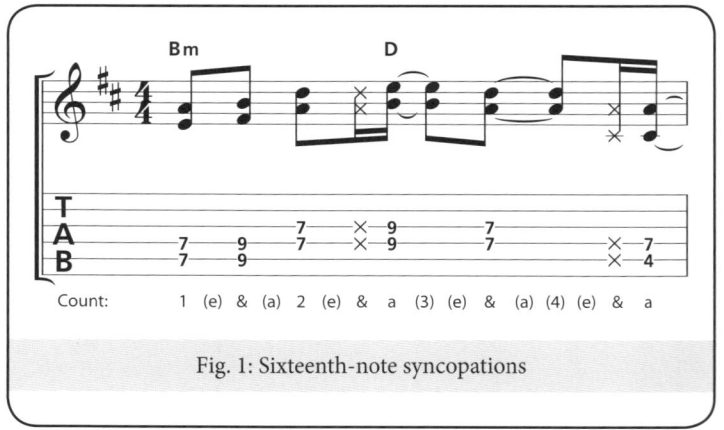

Fig. 1: Sixteenth-note syncopations

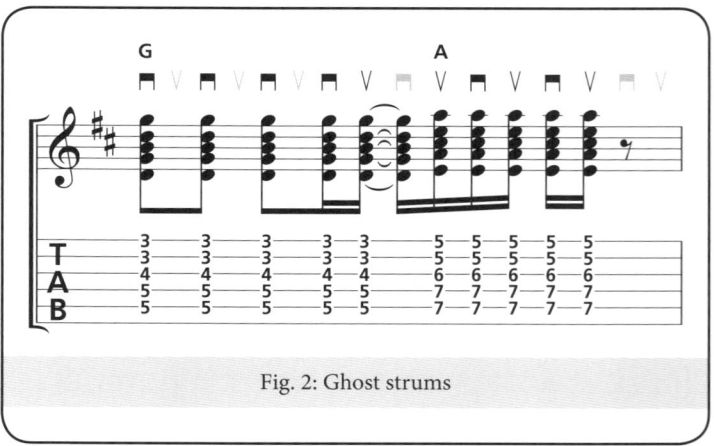

Fig. 2: Ghost strums

Do Balanço

SONG TITLE: DO BALANÇO
GENRE: SAMBA ROCK
TEMPO: 160 BPM
KEY: G MINOR

TECH FEATURES: OCTAVE MELODIES
DOUBLE-STOPS
PLAYING OVER CHANGES

COMPOSER: NOAM LEDERMAN

PERSONNEL: NOAM LEDERMAN (DRUMS)
HENRY THOMAS (BASS)
STUART RYAN (GTR)
KISHON KHAN (KEYS)
FERGUS GERRAND (PERC)

OVERVIEW

'Do Balanço' is in the style of Brazilian artists like Jorge Ben Jor, Trio Mocotó and Clube Do Balanço. It includes techniques such as octave melodies, double-stops and playing over chord changes.

STYLE FOCUS

Samba rock takes its lead from jazz, funk and, of course, samba. Rhythm guitar is generally either funk oriented with tight 16th-note strumming patterns, or played in a syncopated Brazilian style with its roots in bossa nova and samba. Samba lead guitar is influenced mostly by jazz.

THE BIGGER PICTURE

A fusion of samba, rock, soul and jazz, this genre was created in Brazil in the 1960s. The musician Ben Jor pioneered many of these stylistic mixtures in his early albums and is therefore considered to be the father of samba rock and one of the most important figures in the history of Brazilian music. His composition 'Mas Que Nada' became an international hit for Sérgio Mendes and the Black Eyed Peas, and was used as the anthem of the 2006 FIFA World Cup.

Another noteworthy act was Banda Black Rio, who formed in 1976. On their 1977 debut album, *Maria Fumaça,* they mixed samba with jazz funk and soul, inspired by Kool And The Gang and many others. They have since worked with a variety of singers including Caetano Veloso and Gilberto Gil.

Today samba rock is still alive and kicking. Its greatest exponents are arguably the São Paulo group, Clube do Balanço. The band, formed in 1999, have continually propelled the sound created by the masters of samba rock in the 1960s and 1970s into a new fusion that includes dancers, singers, DJs, musicians and producers.

RECOMMENDED LISTENING

As the creator of samba rock, Jorge Ben Jor is worth investigating over several albums: *África Brasil* (1976), *Alô Alô, Como Vai?* (1980) and *A Tábua De Esmeralda* (1974). Bebeto's album *Bebeto* (2005) shows the influence of Ben Jor as Bebeto continued to develop samba rock. Mocotó's *Trio Mocotó* (1973) and Banda Black Rio's *Maria Fumaça* (1977) are examples of samba rock in the 1970s, while Clube Do Balanço's *Swing & Samba-Rock* (2001) illustrates how the genre has evolved even further.

Do Balanço

Noam Lederman

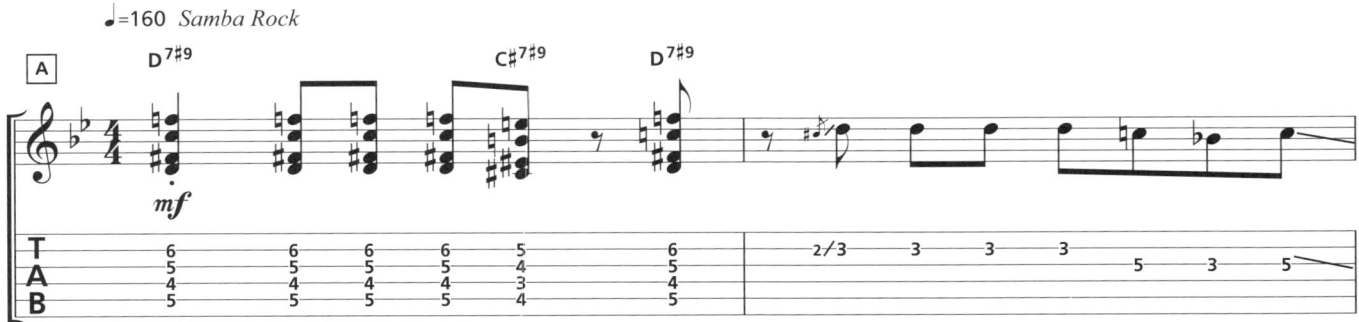
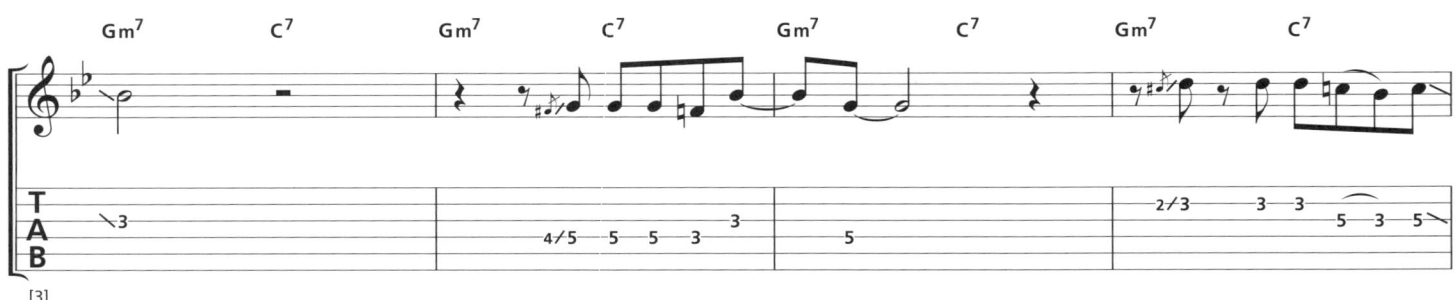
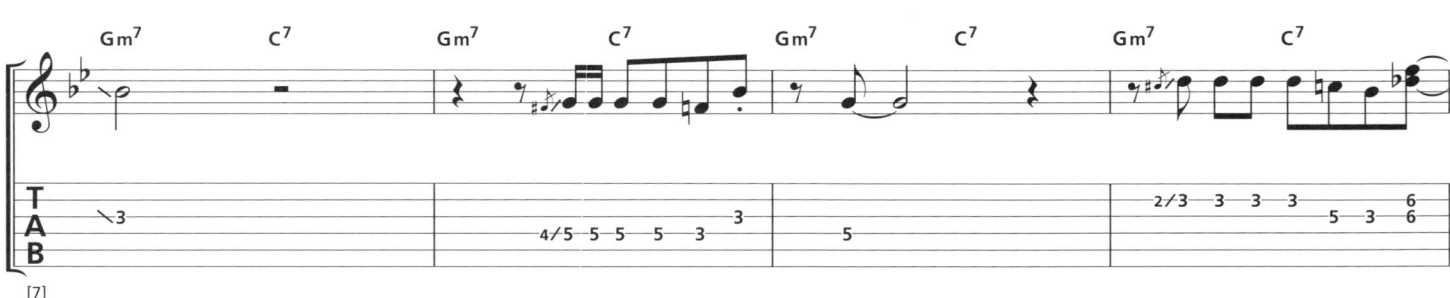
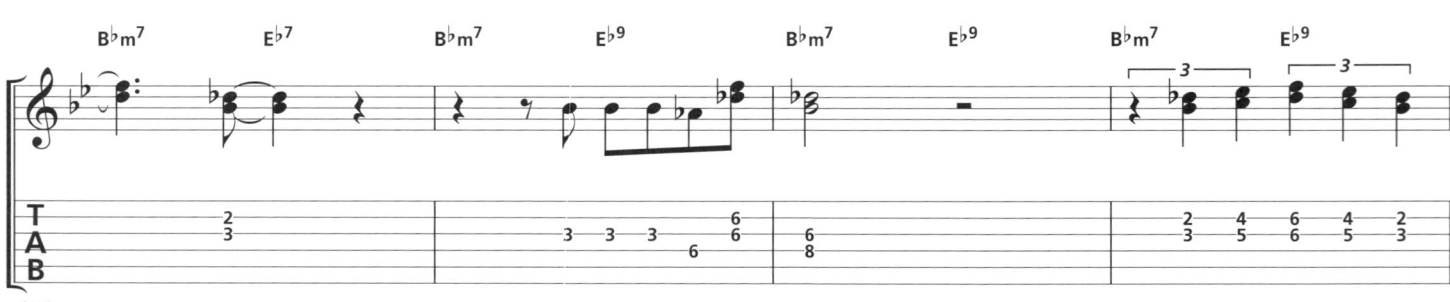

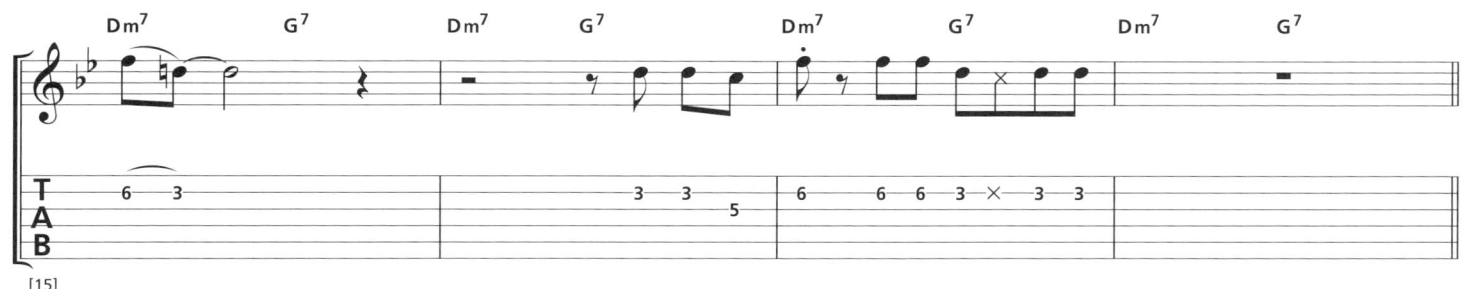
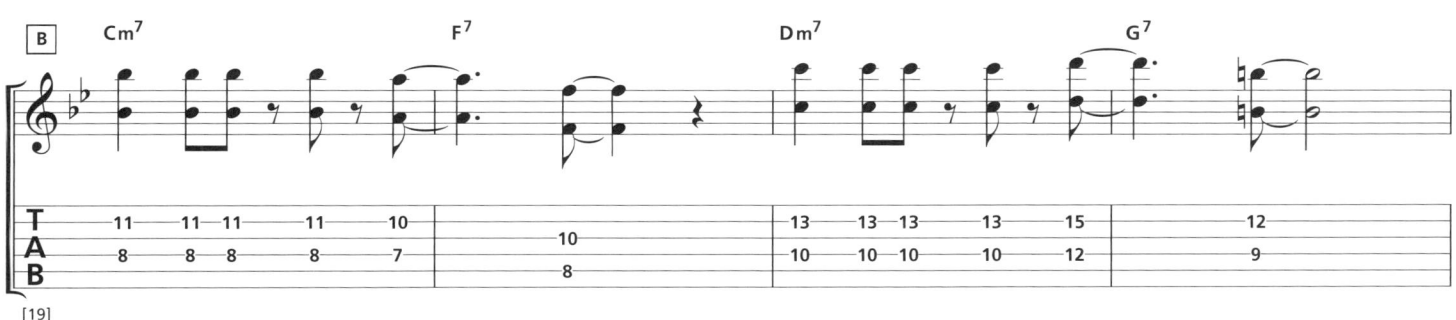
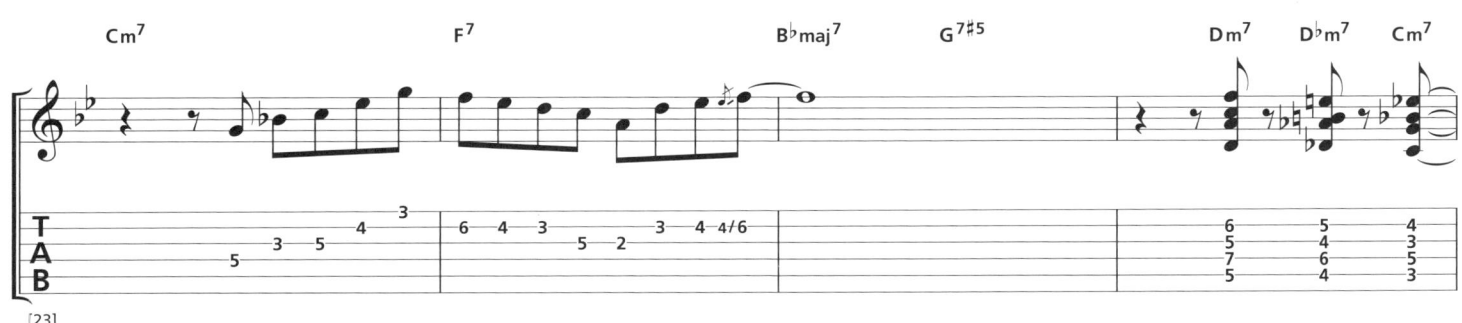
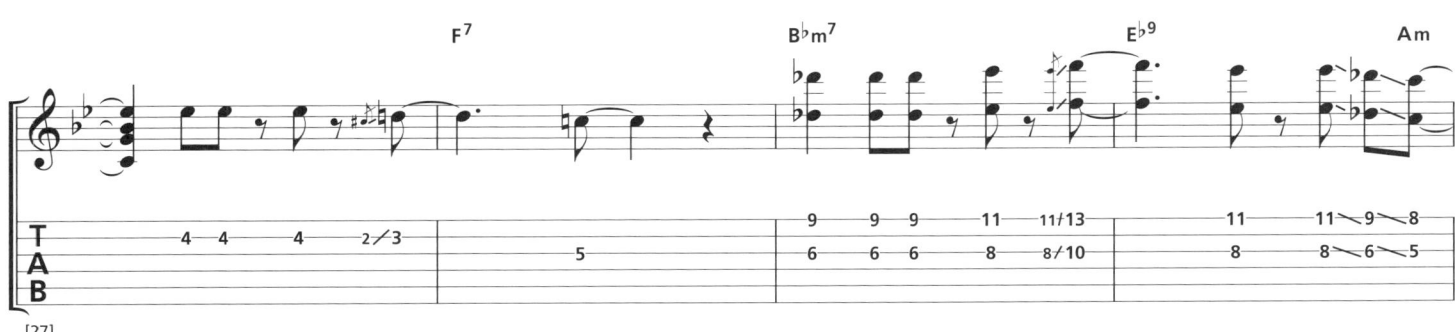

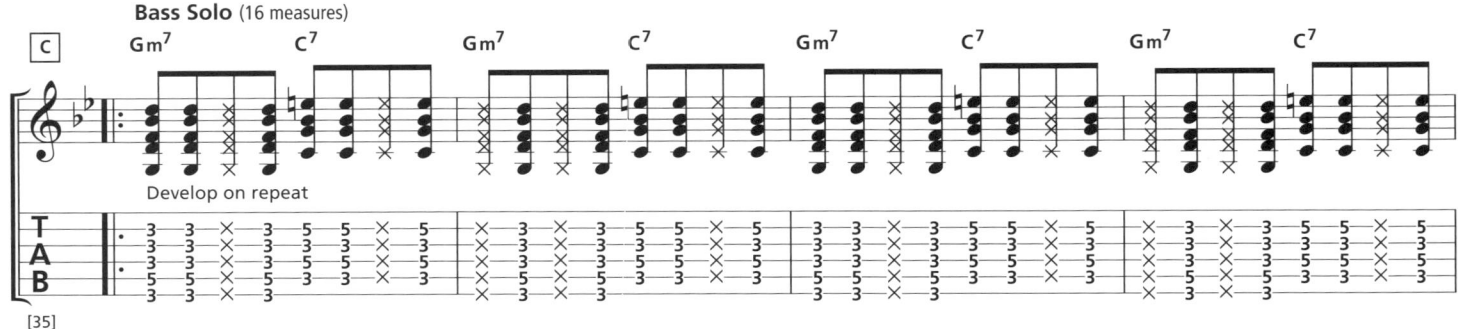
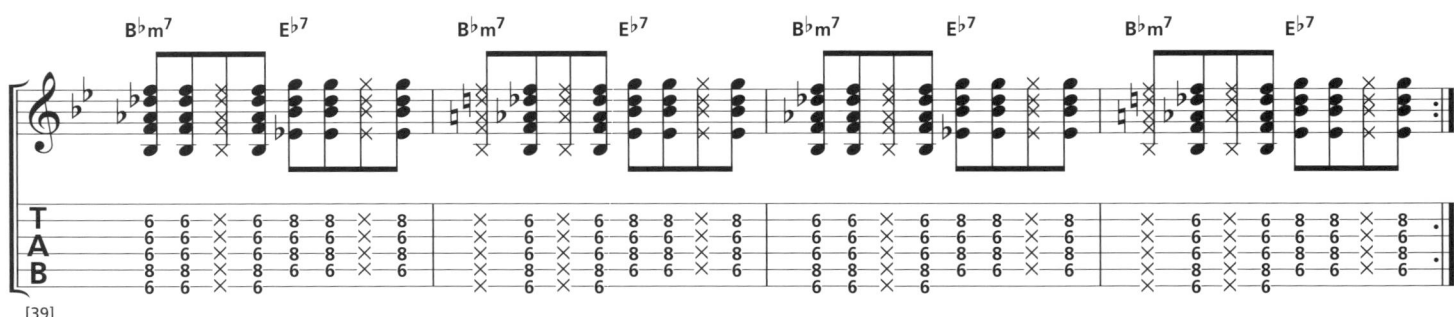
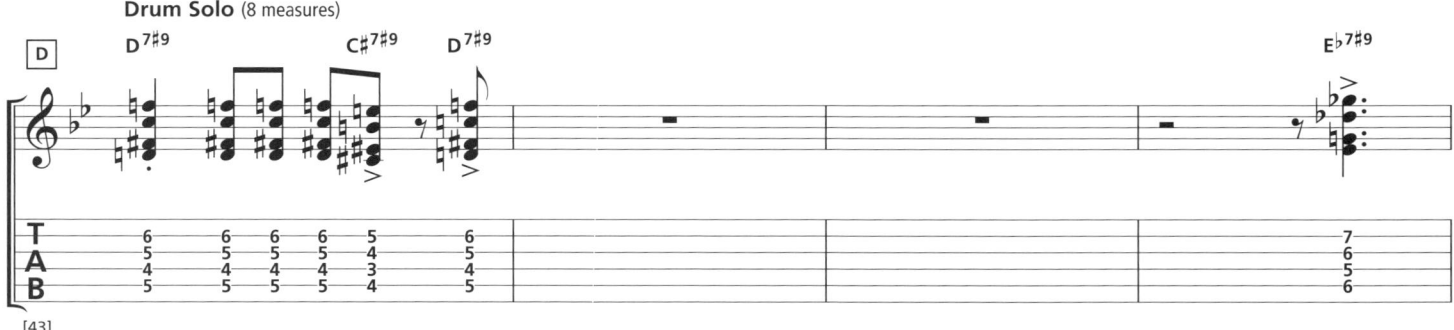
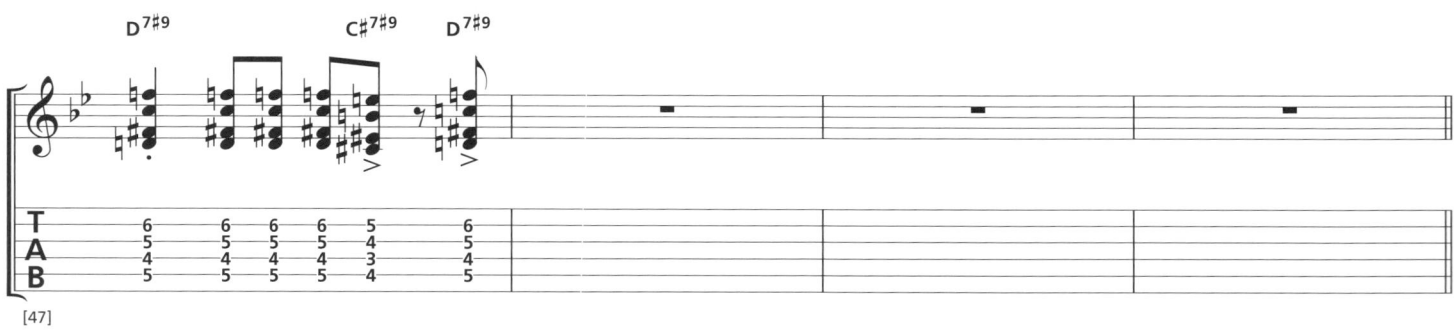
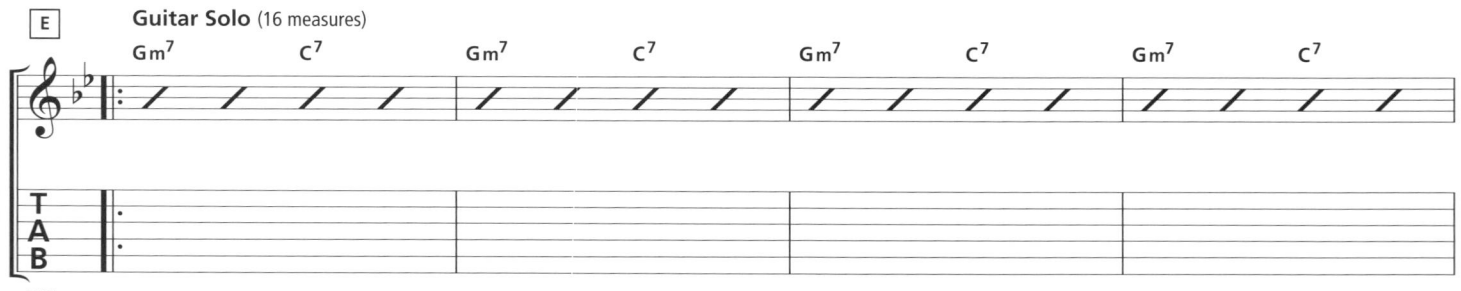

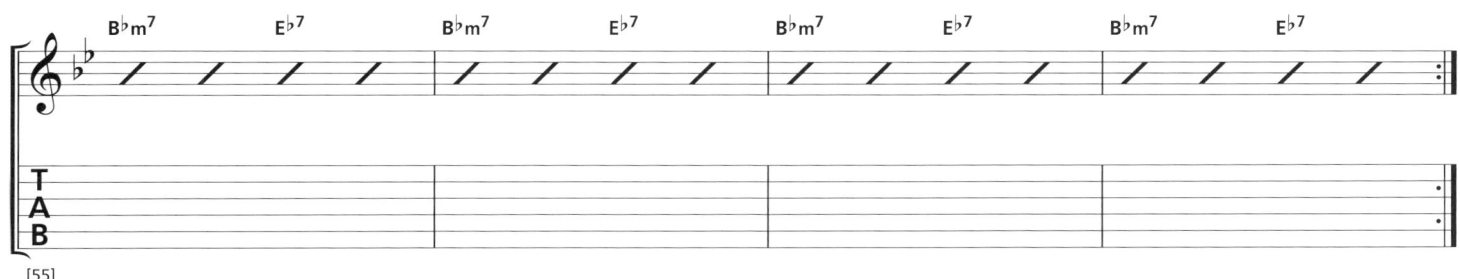
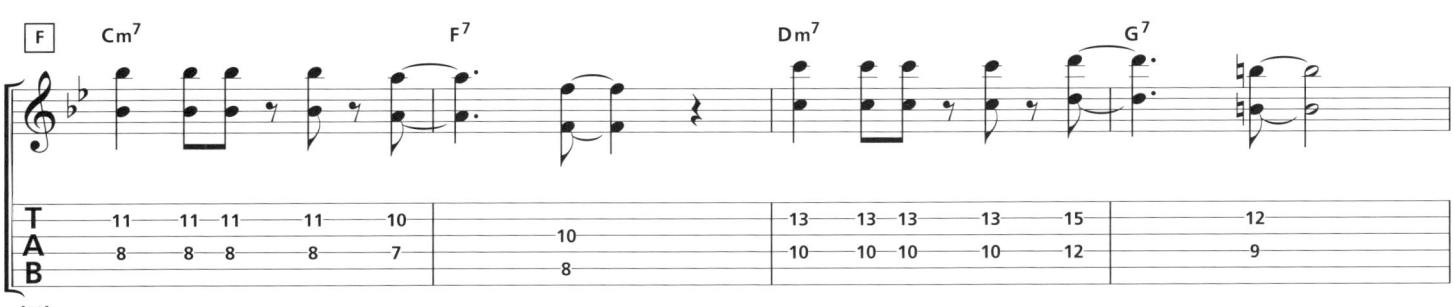
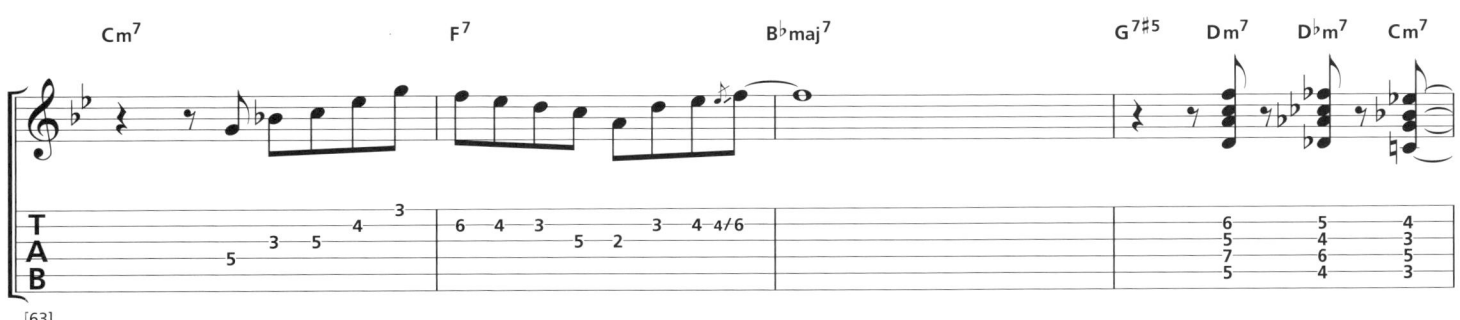
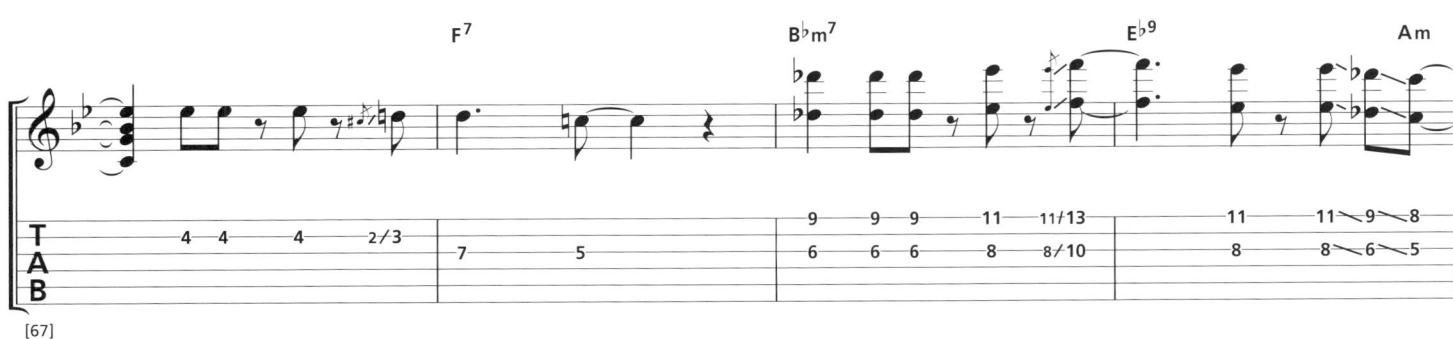

Walkthrough

Amp Settings

Aim for a clean tone that's full and warm. Using your guitar's neck pickup will help with this. Boost the bass (but don't let the sound become muddy) and roll off the middle and treble if you feel the sound is too harsh. Adding reverb, if available, will enhance the mood of the piece.

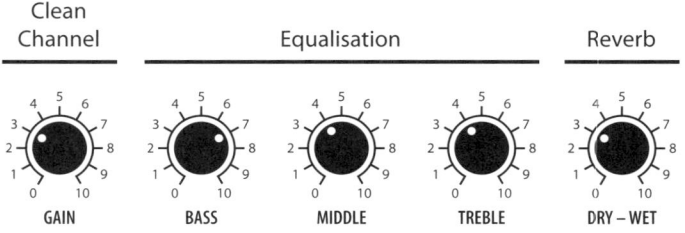

A Section (Measures 1–18)

The song opens with the band playing stabs in unison. The guitar plays a relaxed single-note melody that uses slides, pull-offs and occasional double-stops.

Measures 1–18 | *Starting phrases on the upbeat*
Many of the phrases here start on an upbeat (when you count '&'). At this tempo it can be tricky to play these notes on the right beat or without rushing them. This is especially true of the phrases that start with a grace note. Practise each phrase slowly, counting as you go, and start exactly on the correct beat. Increase the speed when you're ready (Fig. 1).

B Section (Measures 19–34)

The bulk of the B section is based on flowing octave melodies, but there are also several offbeat chord stabs.

Measures 29–32 | *Sliding octaves*
Approach sliding octaves in the same way you play power and barre chords: lock your fingers in position and move the fretting hand as a unit rather than dealing with individual finger placement. The added difficulty of sliding octaves is that you must maintain pressure on the strings to keep the notes ringing. You should feel as if you're pushing into the fretboard as well as sliding up or down to a new fret. This may take some practice to get right, especially if you use the weaker fourth finger to fret the higher octave (Fig. 2).

C Section (Measures 35–42)

This is the bass solo. You should play the written notation first time through then develop the part on the repeat.

Measures 35–42 | *Developing a part*
When you develop a part, make sure you are faithful to the original notated part while still taking the section somewhere new. Common ways to develop a part are to vary the rhythm and picking patterns or use different chord voicings. These are, of course, only suggestions and you should play the part as you feel works best.

D Section (Measures 43–50)

The guitar plays rhythmic stabs in the drum solo. Counting the rests and playing in time is essential in this section.

Measures 43–50 | *Maintaining a pulse*
It's important to tap your foot and/or count the beats through solos. This is especially true of drum solos where drummers may play complex rhythms where the pulse is less obvious.

E & F Sections (Measures 51–73)

The guitar solo starts in G minor then moves to B♭ minor. The F section is a reprise of the A section.

Measures 51–58 | *Scale choices*
The G minor pentatonic scale and G blues scales are good choices for the first four measures of the guitar solo, while the B♭ minor pentatonic and blues scales will work for the second four measures. The G and B♭ dorian modes are more advanced scale choices.

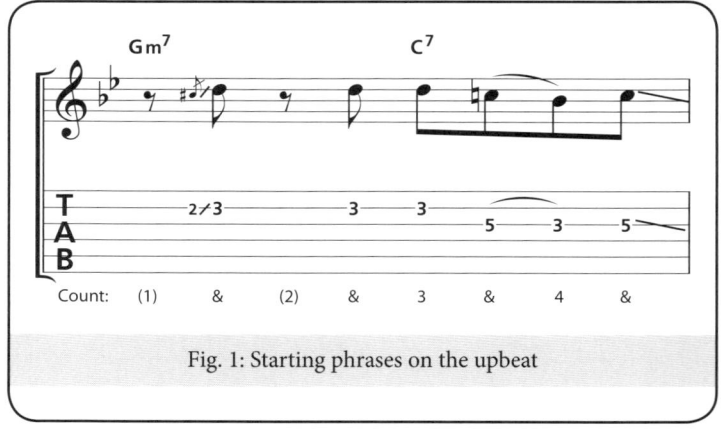

Fig. 1: Starting phrases on the upbeat

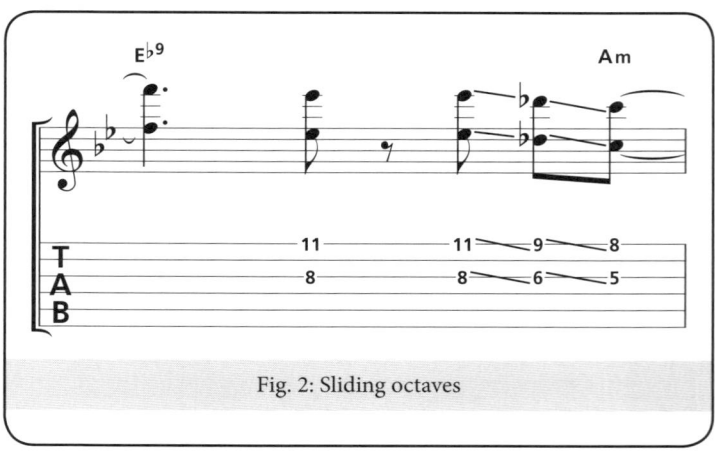

Fig. 2: Sliding octaves

Tiberius

SONG TITLE: TIBERIUS
GENRE: METAL
TEMPO: 90 BPM
KEY: E MINOR

TECH FEATURES: ARPEGGIATED CHORDS
NATURAL HARMONICS
SCALE SEQUENCES

COMPOSERS: CHARLIE GRIFFITHS
& JASON BOWLD

PERSONNEL: CHARLIE GRIFFITHS (GTR)
DAVE MARKS (BASS)
JASON BOWLD (DRUMS)

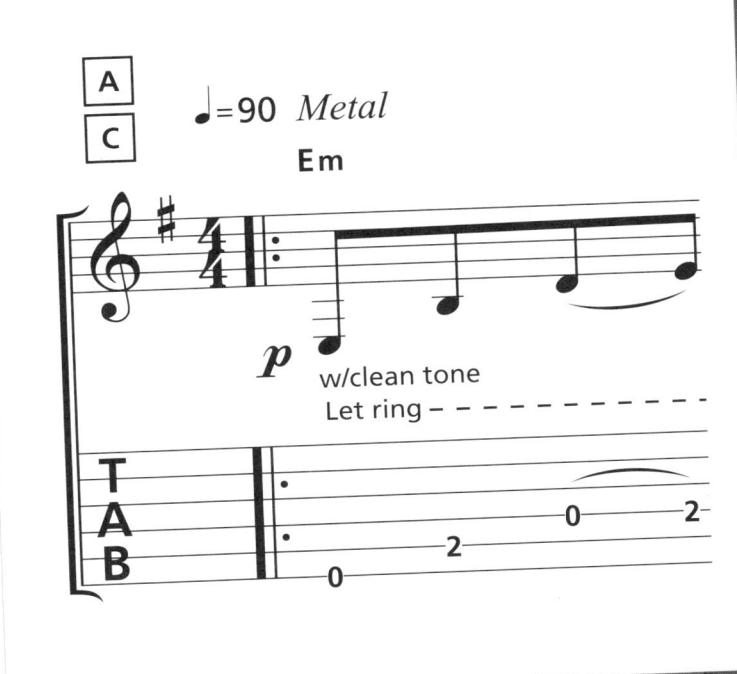

OVERVIEW

'Tiberius' is in the style of Metallica, Exodus and Anthrax, and starts with some mellow arpeggiated chords using open strings and natural harmonics. The next section, based on the E minor pentatonic scale, is played with distortion. Make sure you're comfortable with counting the 2/4 measure because this section also doubles as the solo section backing. After the solo, the feel changes into a more upbeat thrash groove and moves between the keys of E minor and F# minor.

STYLE FOCUS

Thrash is built mainly on the 'root 5th' powerchord, played with a thick distorted sound and an emphasis on percussive, palm-muted low chugging riffs. The rhythmic structures are usually based on constant eighth or 16th notes using the open E or A strings as pedal notes. Soloing is usually based in pentatonic and blues scales. However, the natural minor scale and phrygian modes are also popular.

THE BIGGER PICTURE

Thrash was created and popularised in America in the 1980s by The Big Four: Metallica, Megadeth, Anthrax and Slayer (although other lesser known bands such as Kreator, Exodus and Annihilator have each contributed important albums that have furthered and added individual dynamics to thrash metal). Almost every metal sub genre, including death metal, metalcore, power metal, mathcore and progressive metal, owes its existence to the original thrash style. The genre lives on today with newer bands like Trivium and Avenged Sevenfold harking back to the classic Metallica style while still managing to sound fresh and relevant.

RECOMMENDED LISTENING

Between the mid 1980s and early 1990s, Metallica released a trio of classic thrash albums. *Master of Puppets* (1986) was the first sign of the group's maturing, a process that helped thrash to develop into a genre that could encompass a broad sweep of emotions and musical motifs. *…And Justice For All* (1988) offered more of the same, while their eponymous 1991 LP unleased thrash into more mainstream territory. Slayer's *Reign In Blood* (1986), Exodus' *Bonded By Blood* (1985) and Megadeth's *Rust In Peace* (1990) are all great examples from the same period. More currently, Avenged Sevenfold's *Nightmare* (2010) has some classic Metallica-esque moments, as does Trivium's 2011 *In Waves*.

Tiberius

Charlie Griffiths & Jason Bowld

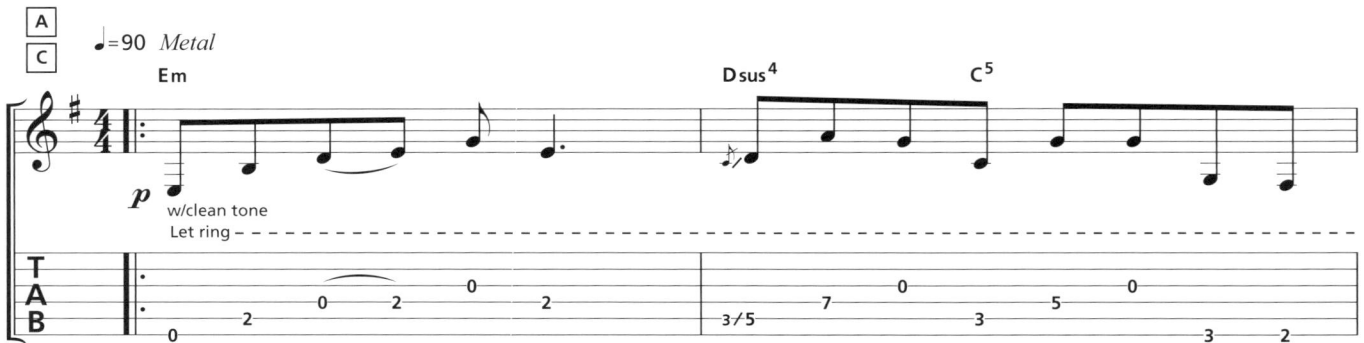
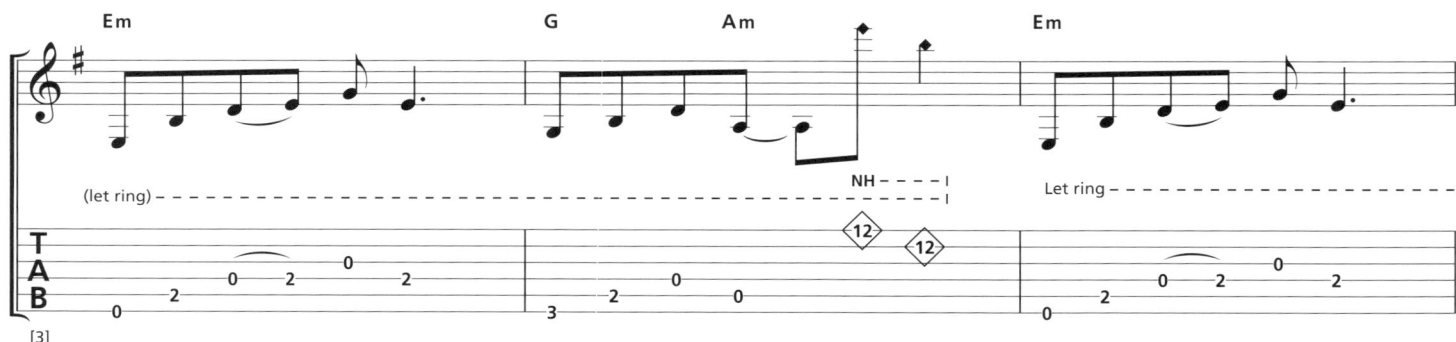

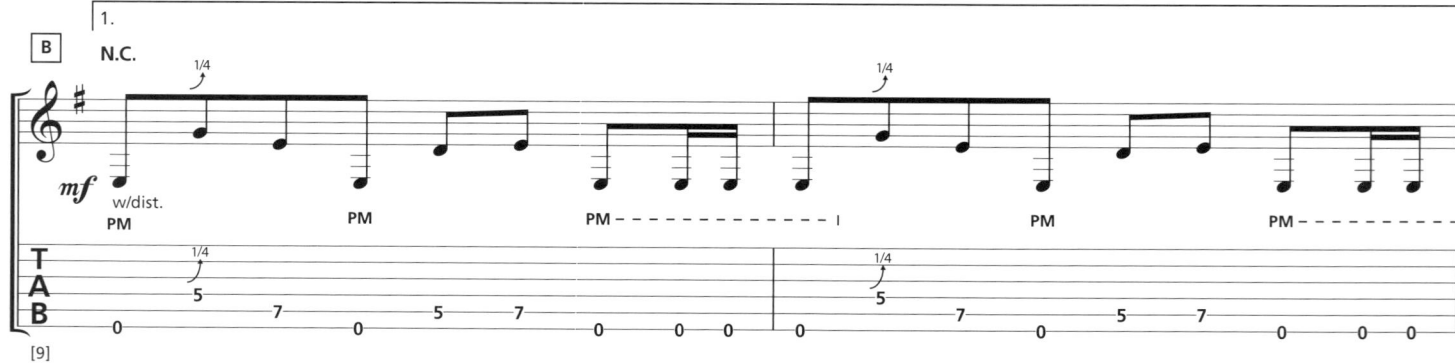

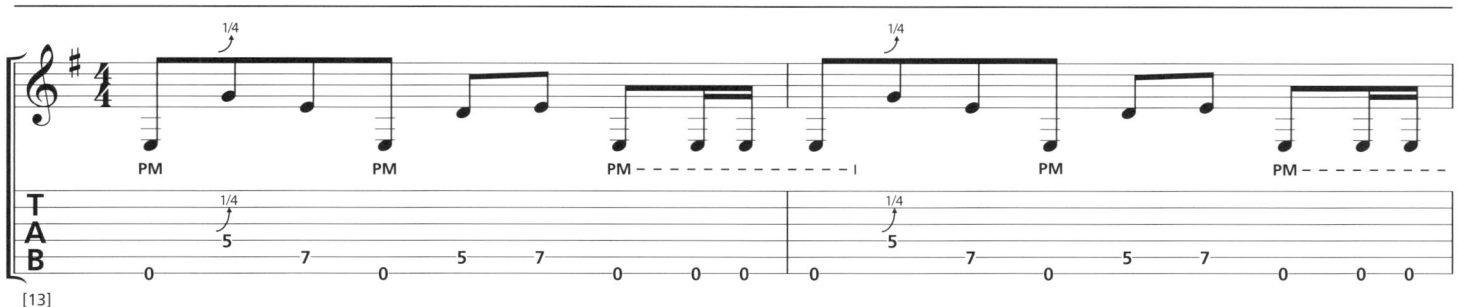
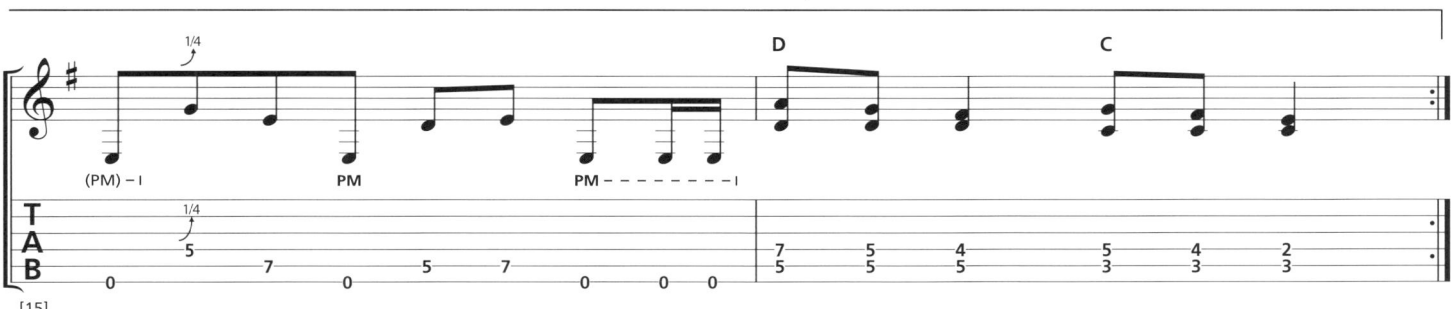
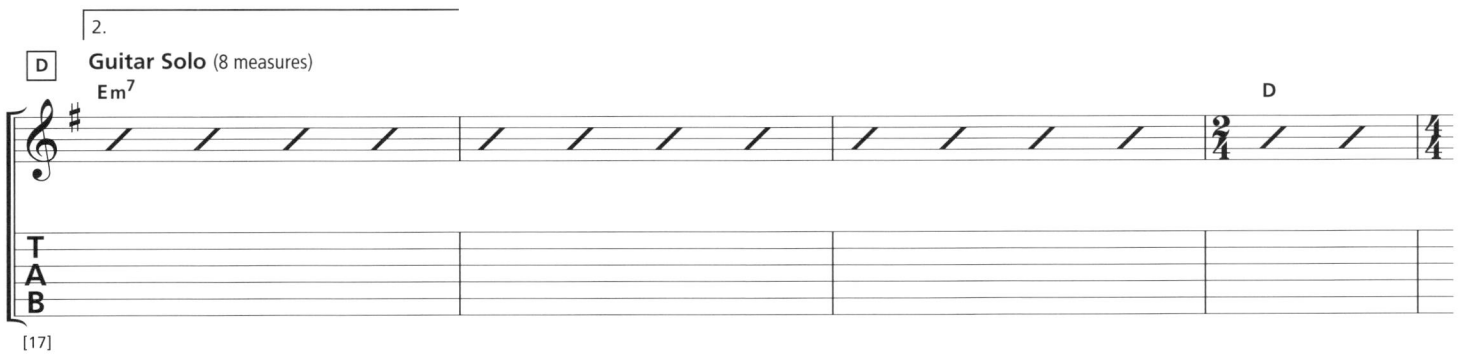
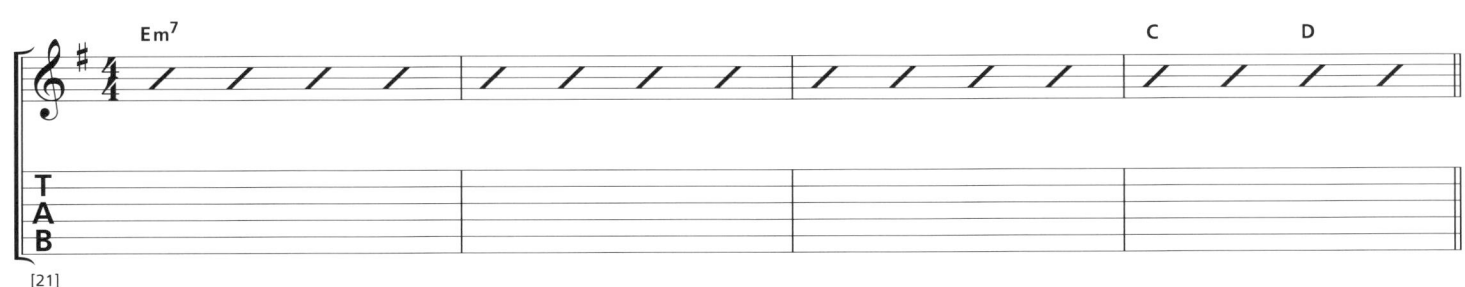

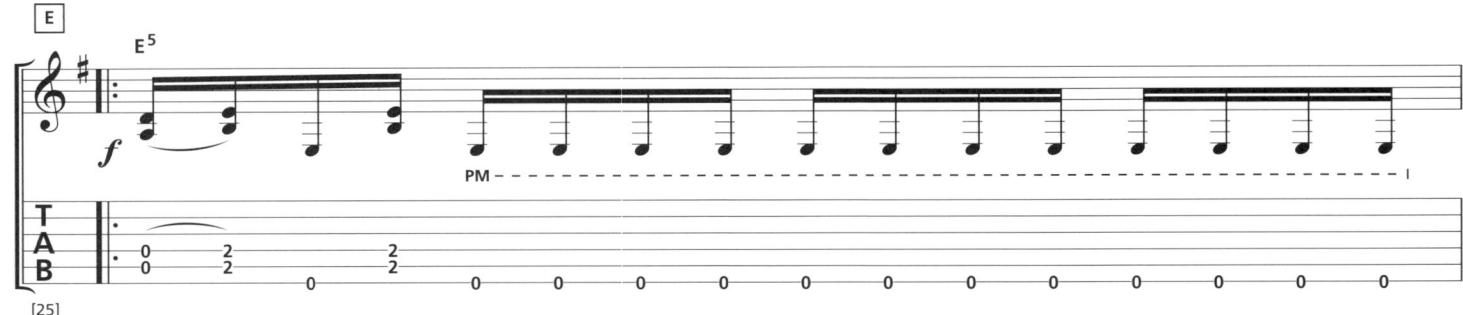
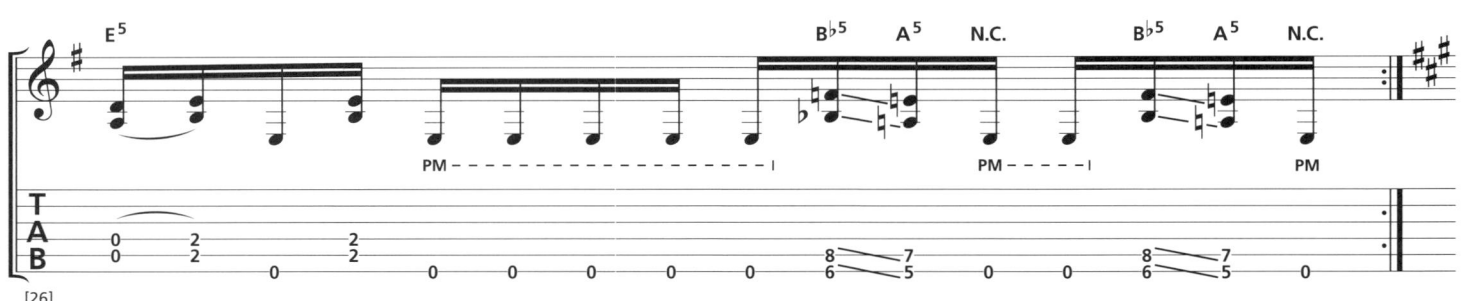
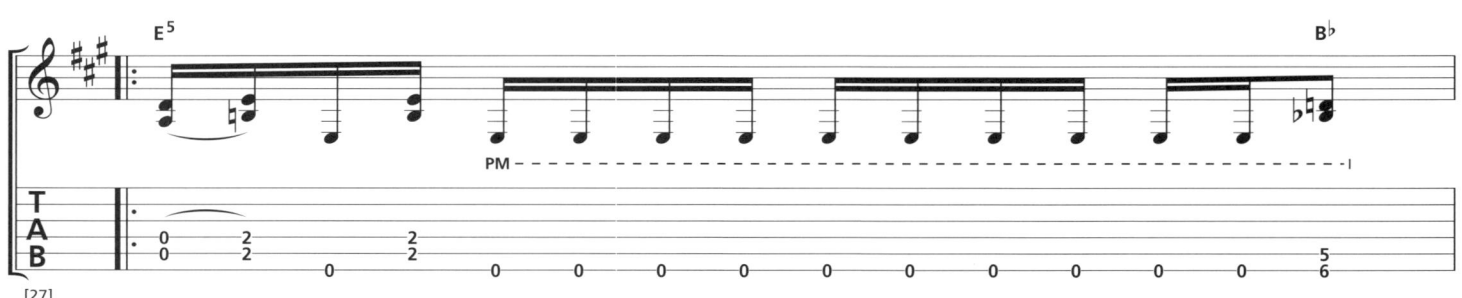
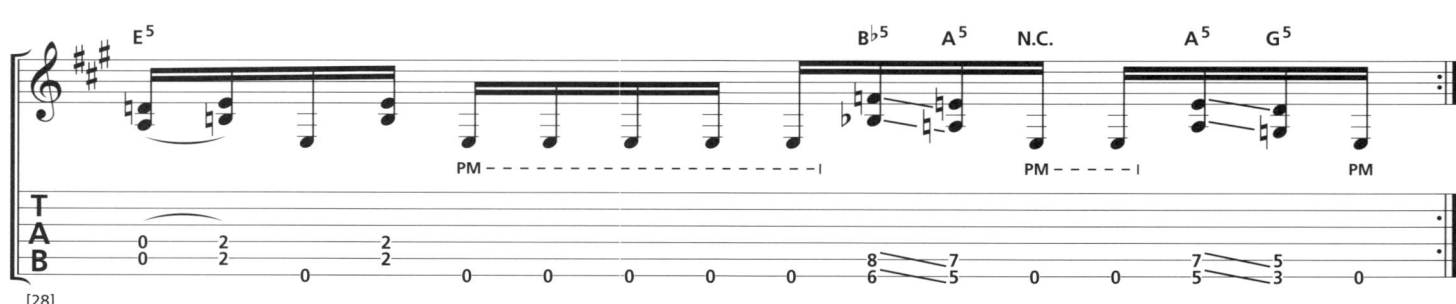
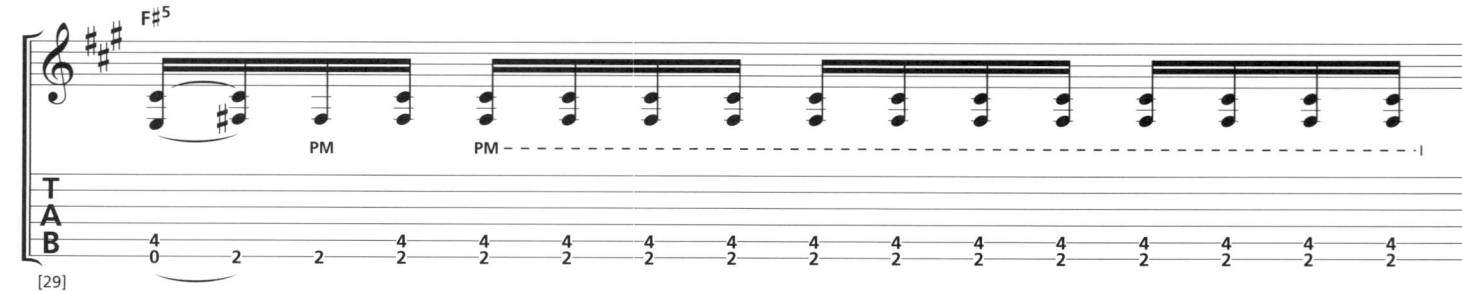

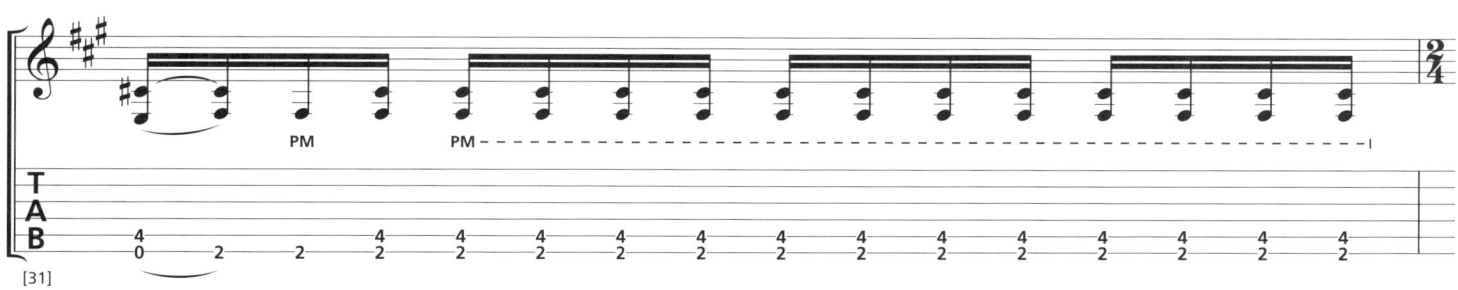
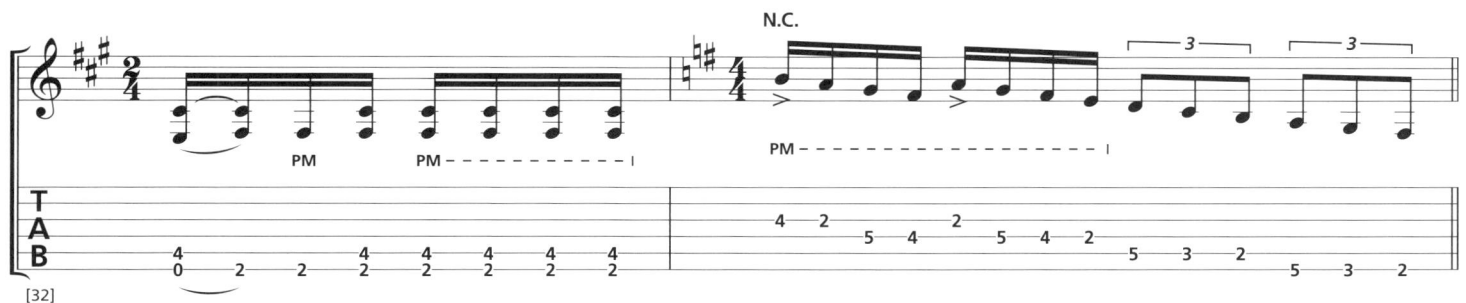
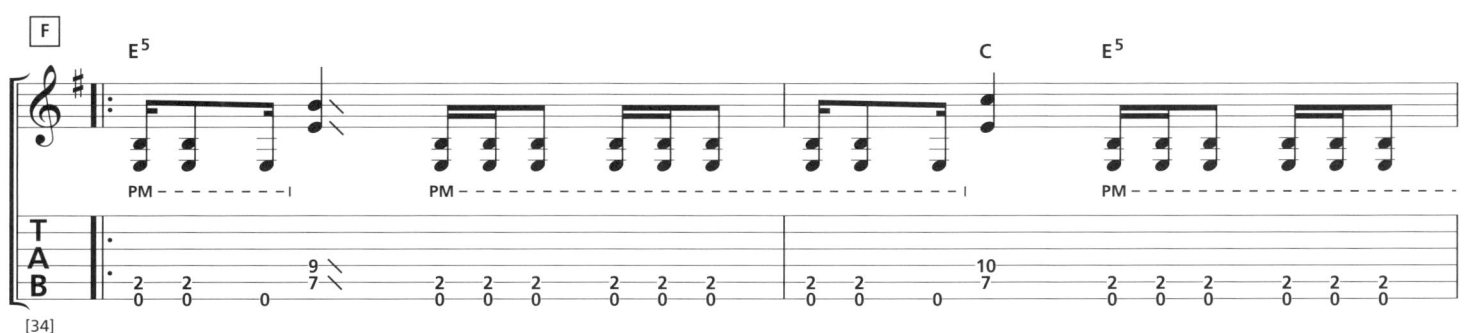
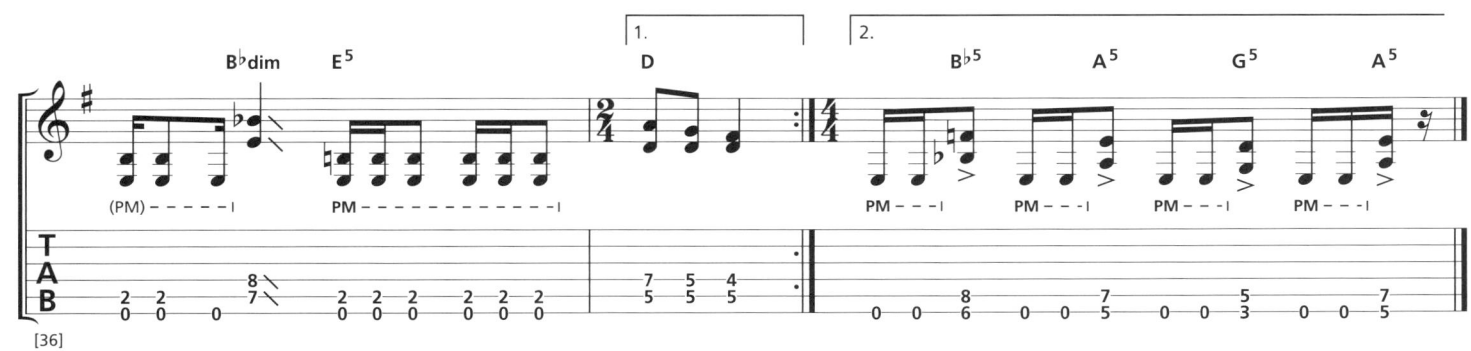

Walkthrough

Amp Settings
This song requires both clean and distorted tones. A metal guitar tone consists of two elements: modern high-gain distortion and a scooped tone. A scooped tone is achieved by boosting the treble and bass controls and cutting or 'scooping out' the middle. If you are using an effects pedal for both sounds, make sure the balance is correct between the two tones. Generally speaking, the clean tone will be slightly quieter than distortion.

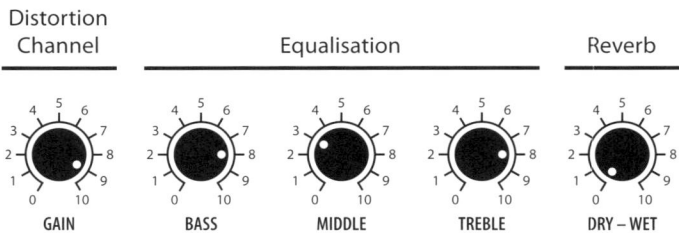

A & C Section (Measures 1–8)
The A section consists of arpeggiated chords where all the notes ring for as long as possible. The C section is a repeat of the A section, but this time the bass takes a solo.

Measure 4 | *Natural harmonics*
Natural harmonics are sounded by lightly placing your finger directly over the frets. Don't make contact with the any part of the fretboard here, otherwise this will choke the notes (Fig. 1).

Measure 8 | *Changing tones*
You must change from a clean tone in the A section to a distorted tone in the B section. There is a one-and-a-half beat gap from striking the last note of the A section to the first note of the B section. Use this time to prepare to change tone just before you play the first note of the B section.

B Section (Measures 9–16)
Here you will encounter a classic metal riff that uses the open E string as a pedal tone. Quarter-tone bends and heavy palm-muting contribute to the riff's character.

Measure 12 | *2/4 measure*
You may be thrown by the 2/4 measure at first. Many treat the 2/4 measure and the first half of the next measure as a measure of 4/4. This places the strong beats of the measure (usually beat 1) in the wrong place and can be confusing. Count through the measures to help you feel where each new measure starts (Fig. 2).

D Section (Measures 17–24)
The D section is the guitar solo, which is played over the B section riff. The E minor pentatonic, blues and natural minor scales are ideal for this solo. The natural minor scale will give a darker sound than the other two scales.

E Section (Measures 25–33)
This classic metal riff comprises of two-note chordal riffs mixed with chugging, heavily palm-muted single strings.

Measures 25–33 | *Fast picking*
16th-note picking on the low strings can be quite challenging so start off slowly. Concentrate on a relaxed picking action and look to minimise the distance the pick travels past the string on each pick stroke.

F Section (Measures 34–38)
The F section is a stomping aggressive riff that contrasts low palm-muted notes with higher, un-muted chords.

Measures 34–38 | *Heavy palm-muting*
Place the outside edge of your palm on the lowest sounding strings and press firmly to get the heavy choke required for this part. Be careful not to move your hand too far from the bridge because this may raise the pitch of the note.

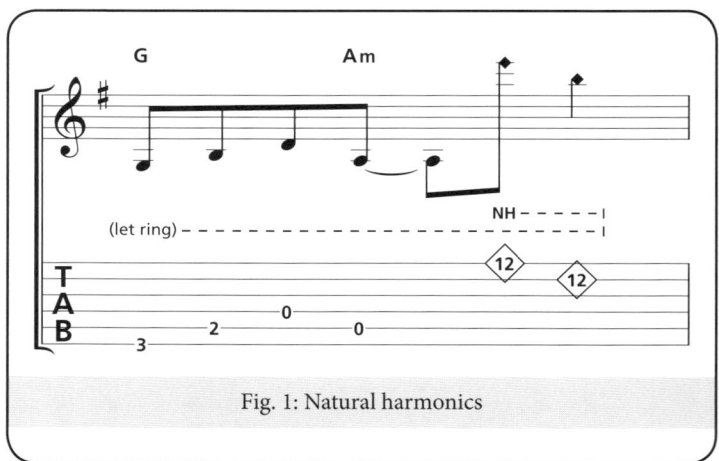

Fig. 1: Natural harmonics

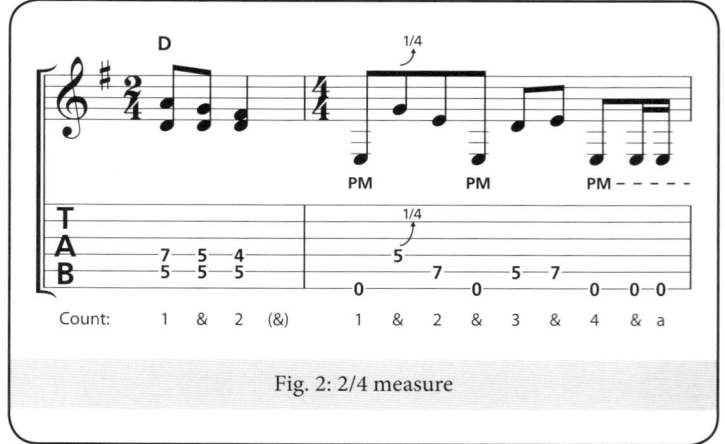

Fig. 2: 2/4 measure

Smack Talk

SONG TITLE: SMACK TALK
GENRE: BLUES ROCK
TEMPO: 115 BPM
KEY: G MINOR

TECH FEATURES: TRIPLET RHYTHMS
ALTERNATE PICKING
AGGRESSIVE SOLOING

COMPOSER: SIMON TROUP

PERSONNEL: STUART RYAN (GTR)
HENRY THOMAS (BASS)
NOAM LEDERMAN (DRUMS)
ROSS STANLEY (KEYS)

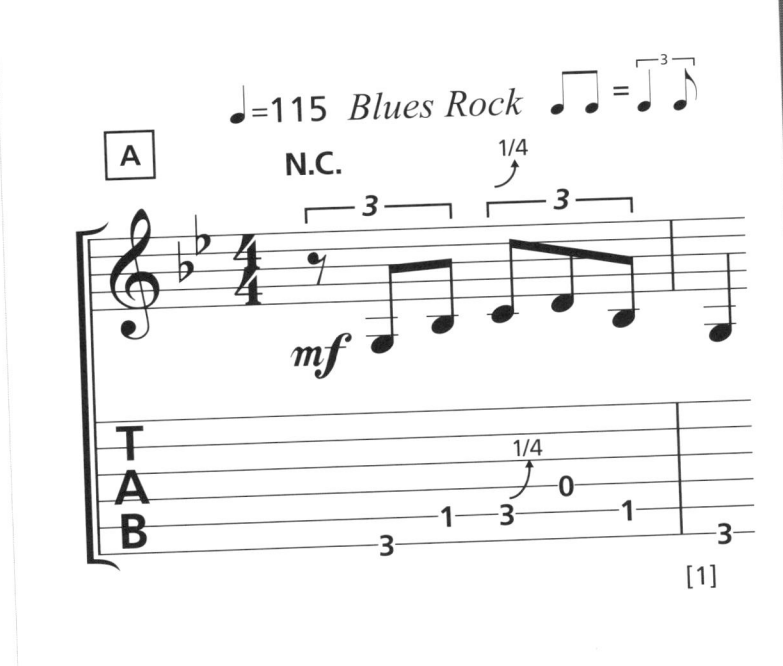

OVERVIEW

'Smack Talk' is a modern blues rock composition inspired by Joe Bonamassa and Gary Moore. This mid tempo track features the swagger and attack typical of this style, along with a thickly distorted tone commonly found in blues rock. In this style it is normal for the solo to take more of a heavy rock character with faster lines and a hard attack.

STYLE FOCUS

Blues rock developed from the late 1960s onwards as the influence of bands like Cream and The Jimi Hendrix Experience started to trickle down to the next generation of bands. Groups like Deep Purple took the I–IV–V format of the blues and developed minor pentatonic based riffs around it. This was interspersed with chordal ideas (often dominant sevenths) and a heavier, more distorted guitar sound in keeping with the amplifiers that now allowed guitarists a greater range of tones.

THE BIGGER PICTURE

Bonamassa, like Moore before him, uses a Gibson Les Paul to produce the most saturated, sustain-heavy guitar tone possible. Moore came to prominence as a guitarist for Thin Lizzy in the 1970s, and later become a successful solo artist who based his playing and songwriting on the blues. His melding of the two genres resulted in a heavily distorted sound and pyrotechnical displays of fretboard virtuosity that are common with the majority of rock players. Bonamassa is a popular modern blues rock guitarist renowned for his tone, riff writing and technical ability. He is first and foremost a blues guitarist with an innate knowledge of the style: in his early teens he played with many blues legends including B.B. King.

RECOMMENDED LISTENING

Classic Gary Moore tracks are 'Walking By Myself', 'Parisienne Walkways' and his emotive 'Still Got The Blues', although there are many other gems in his back catalogue. To begin, try the live album *Blues Alive* (1993) where you can hear him play classic blues alongside Albert Collins, a wonderful sustained version of 'Still Got The Blues' and fiery licks on 'Walking By Myself'. Joe Bonamassa's own output is prolific, with a heavy touring schedule to match. Bonamassa's modern take on the blues rock sound can be heard on *You And Me* (2006), while *Live At The Royal Albert Hall* (2010) demonstrates his superb command of the guitar.

Smack Talk

Simon Troup

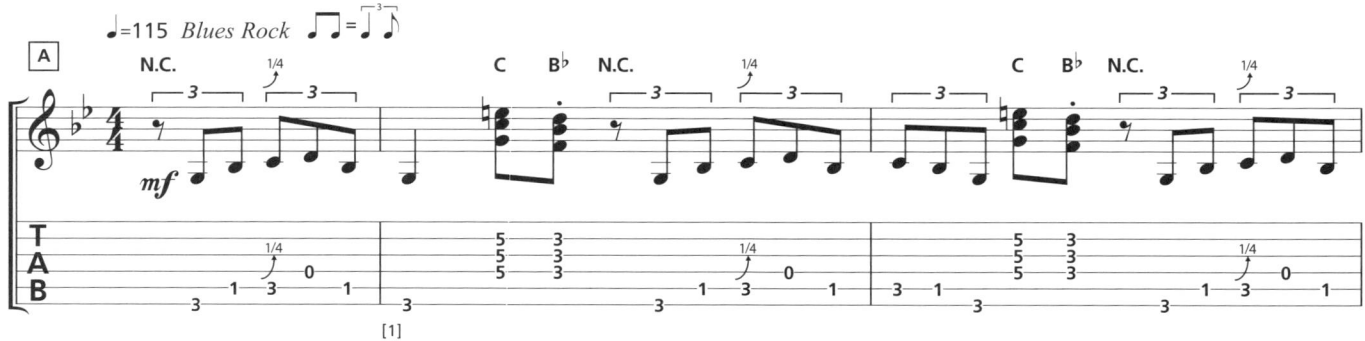

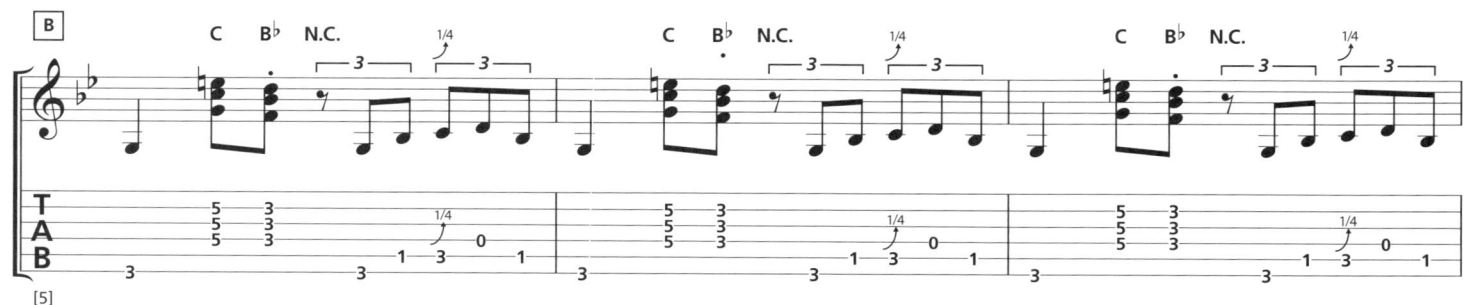
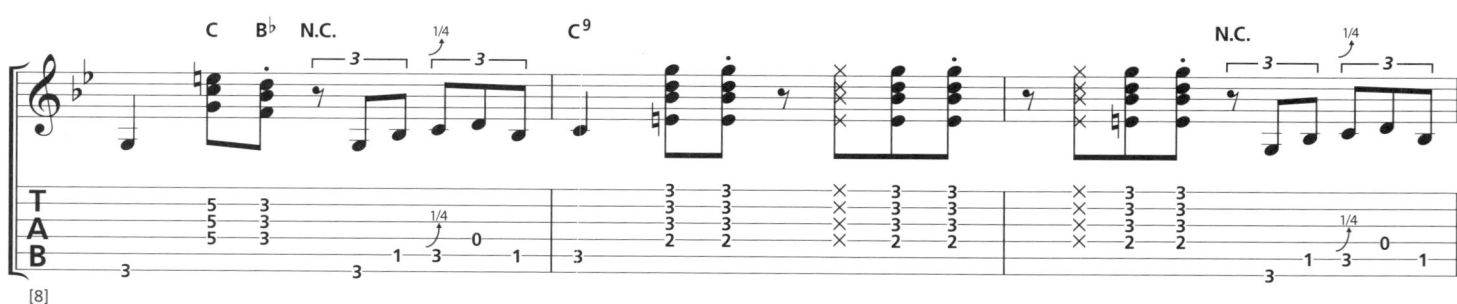
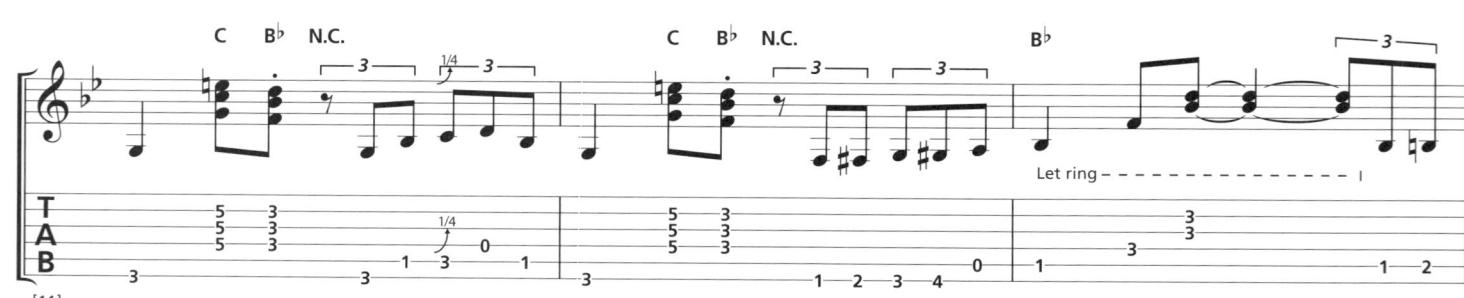

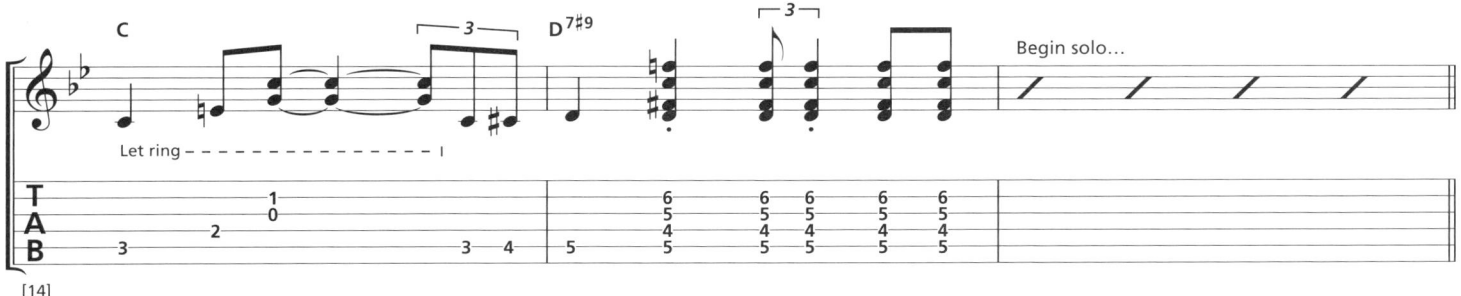

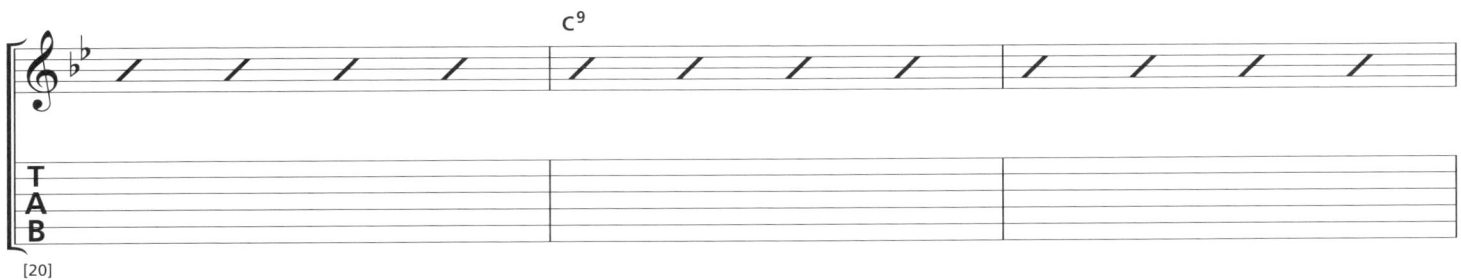

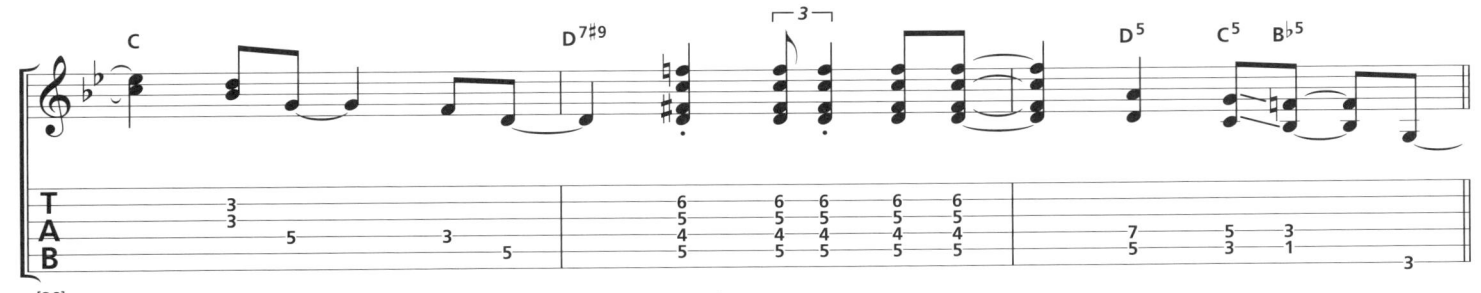

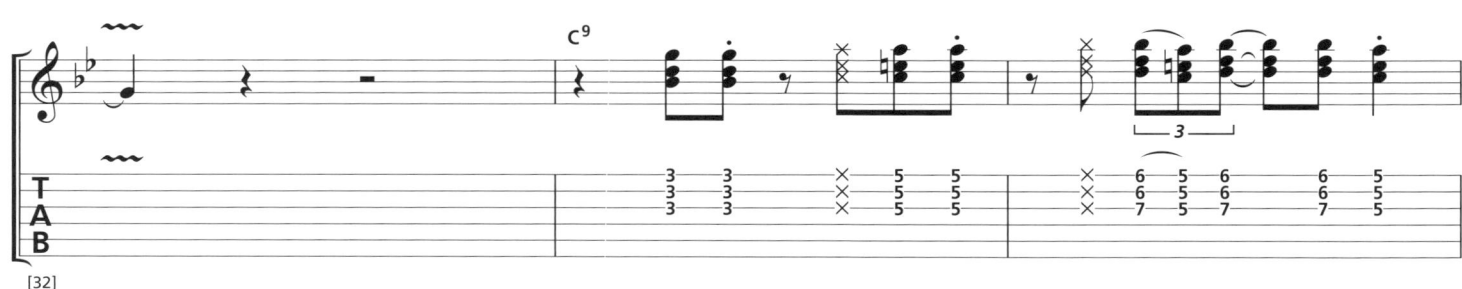
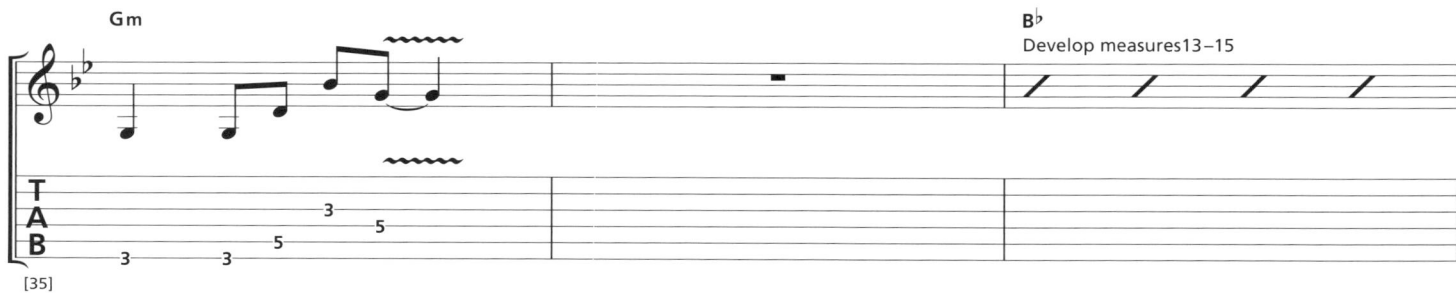
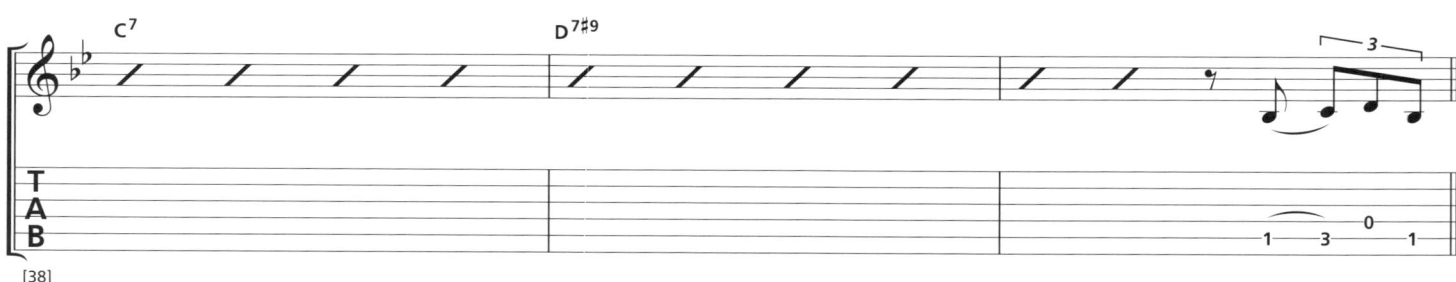

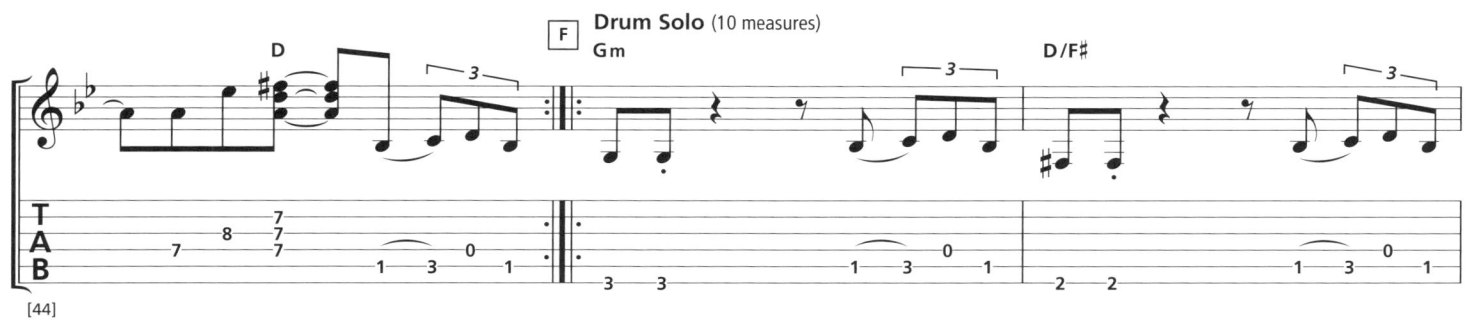

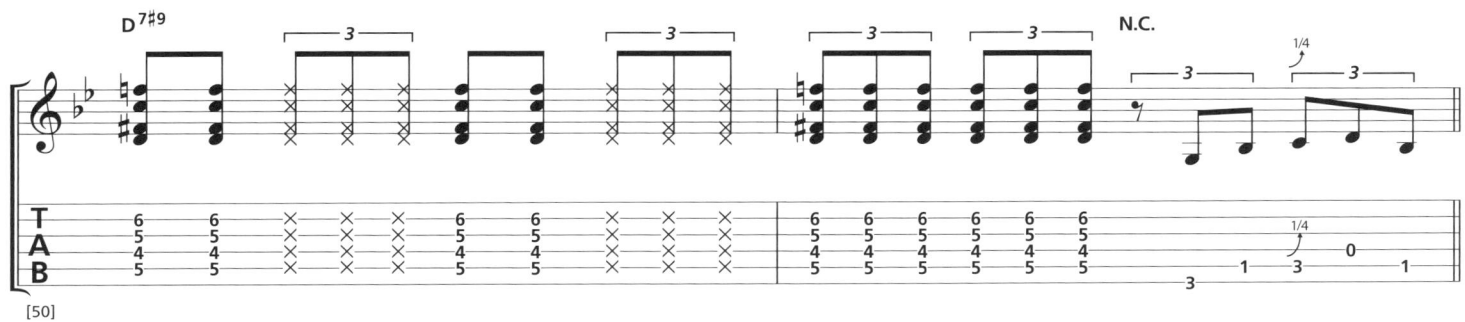

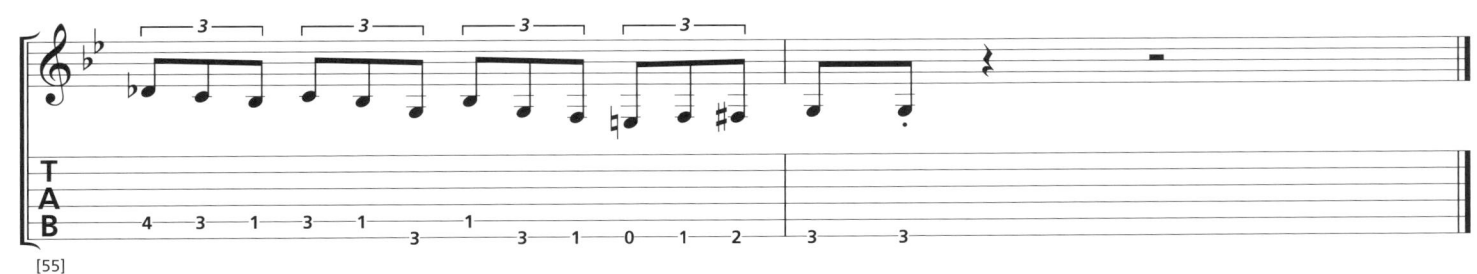

Walkthrough

Amp Settings

Aim for an aggressive overdriven tone with plenty of bite. Set the gain quite high and boost the middle to help the guitar's sound cut through the mix, particularly in the solo – remember though, this is blues rock, not metal. Your bridge pickup will help provide some bite to your tone.

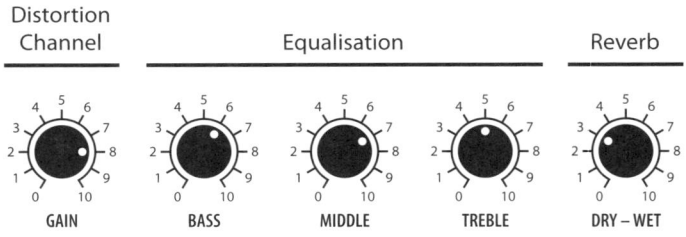

A Section (Measures 1–4)

This is a single-note riff interspersed with chordal stabs.

Pick-up measure | *Starting on an upbeat*
The first note is played on the second note of a triplet, which is hard to play correctly. Count triplets along with the spoken count-in to prepare you for the triplet rhythm so that you can play the first note at the right time (Fig. 1).

Measure 4 | *Alternate picking*
This phrase is difficult to play using any technique other than alternate picking. The trickiest part is crossing between the E and A strings. Focus on this movement and turn it into an exercise (Fig. 2).

B Section (Measures 5–16)

This is a variation of the A section, this time played over a groove. The riff follows a popular blues rock progression.

Measure 9 | *Dominant ^{9} chord*
The dominant ^{9} chord is played by placing your second finger on the 3rd fret of the A string, your first on the 2nd fret of the D string, and the barring the 3rd fret on the remaining strings with your third finger. Check all the notes are fretted correctly by picking the individual notes.

C & D Sections (Measures 17–40)

The guitar solo starts in the last measure of the B section. It is based in G minor. Its final four and a half measures are notated. The D section is the bass solo and portions of it are open for you to develop parts found earlier in the piece.

Measures 17–24 | *Guitar solo*
The G minor pentatonic or G blues scale are ideal choices for this solo. Regardless of the direction you decide to take your solo in, make sure you are in position to play the notes in measure 24. Try to avoid large jumps in register that may interrupt the flow of your performance.

Measures 37–40 | *Developing a part*
Develop the part played in measures 13–15. You could vary the rhythm, picking patterns, or use different chord voicings.

E Section (Measures 41–44)

The E section is a single-note riff where the top note of the line descends chromatically for the first three measures.

Measures 41–44 | *Structured fingerings*
There are several fingering options for this section, so work through the riff to find which one works for you. Pay attention to measures 43 and 44 and the transition from the end of the riff at measure 44 to the start of the repeat in measure 41.

F & G Sections (Measures 45–56)

In the drum solo the guitar part draws from the main riff. The G section is a reprise of the A section.

Measures 45–49 | *Maintaining a pulse*
Always tap your foot and/or count the beats through drum solos, especially complex solos with a less obvious pulse.

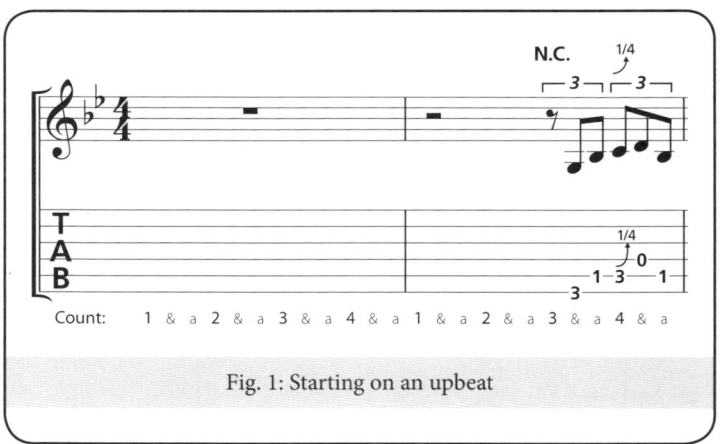

Fig. 1: Starting on an upbeat

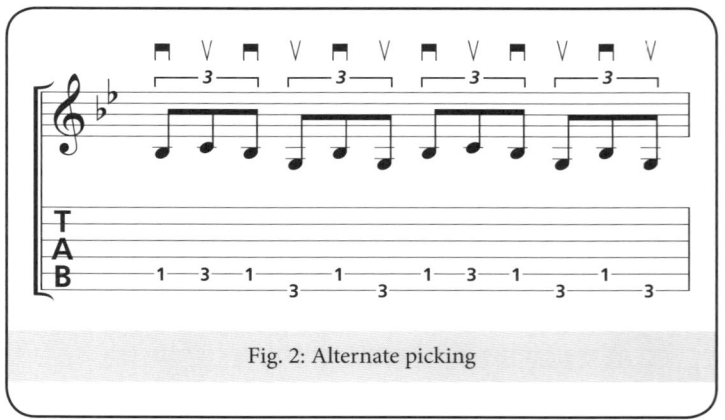

Fig. 2: Alternate picking

Slam Dunk Funk

SONG TITLE: SLAM DUNK FUNK
GENRE: FUNK
TEMPO: 88 BPM
KEY: E MINOR

TECH FEATURES: HAMMER-ONS
SLIDES
NATURAL HARMONICS

COMPOSER: KIT MORGAN

PERSONNEL: KIT MORGAN (GTR)
HENRY THOMAS (BASS)
NOAM LEDERMAN (DRUMS)

OVERVIEW

'Slam Dunk Funk' apes the style of Red Hot Chili Peppers (RHCP), Funkadelic and Sly & The Family Stone, and features hammer-ons, syncopated 16th-note strumming and slides among its techniques.

STYLE FOCUS

As its name suggests, funk rock is a mixture of two styles. From funk we get a strong emphasis on 'the one' (the first beat of each measure) and those distinctive syncopated 16th-note rhythms. The rock influence can be heard in the genre's distorted guitar riffs and solos.

THE BIGGER PICTURE

If James Brown invented funk with his musically radical single 'Cold Sweat' in 1967, Sly Stone is arguably the inventor of funk rock. Stone was leader of the group Sly & The Family Stone who broke down musical barriers with their 1969 album *Stand!*, which combined the dancefloor friendly rhythms of funk with the distorted guitar licks of rock.

At the same time, Jimi Hendrix was becoming a rock guitar hero who incorporated elements of soul and R&B into his music which he had absorbed while touring as a session guitarist with The Isley Brothers.

However inventive and influential Hendrix and Stone were, the funk rock sound was truly defined by George Clinton, who began his recording career as the frontman of a doo-wop vocal group called The Parliaments. In the late 1960s, Clinton discovered the music of Hendrix and Led Zeppelin. He changed course musically and renamed his newly guitar heavy group Funkadelic.

In the 1980s, Clinton produced the RHCP album *Freakey Styley* (1985) and helped steer the band towards their own unique funk rock sound.

RECOMMENDED LISTENING

In 1969, Sly & The Family Stone's *Stand!* fused elements of funk, rock, pop and soul, and guitarist Freddy Stone's distorted guitar tone influenced the sound of many funk and funk rock bands. Funkadelic's *Standing On The Verge Of Getting It On* (1974) is full of tight funk rock riffs and the excellent lead guitar of Eddie Hazel. In the 1990s, RHCP released their most consistently funky album *BloodSugarSexMagik* (1991), a high point in the career of guitarist John Frusciante.

Slam Dunk Funk

Kit Morgan

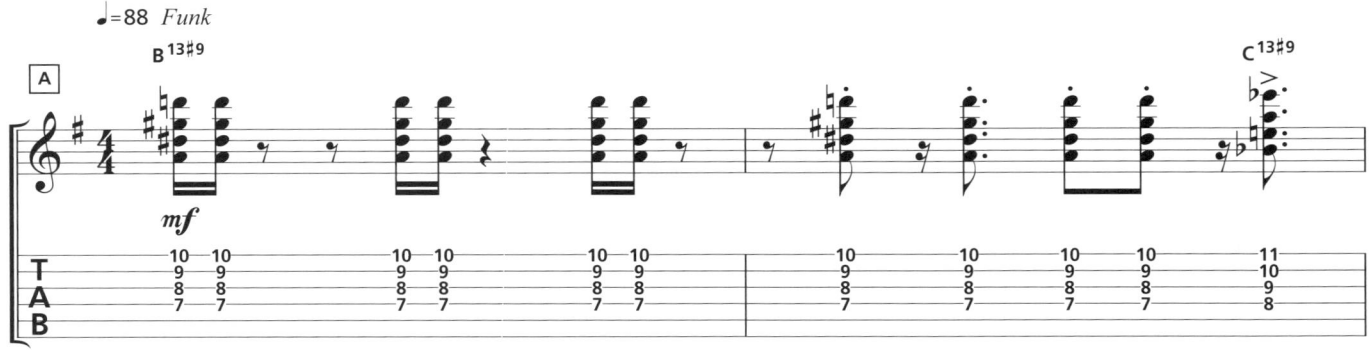
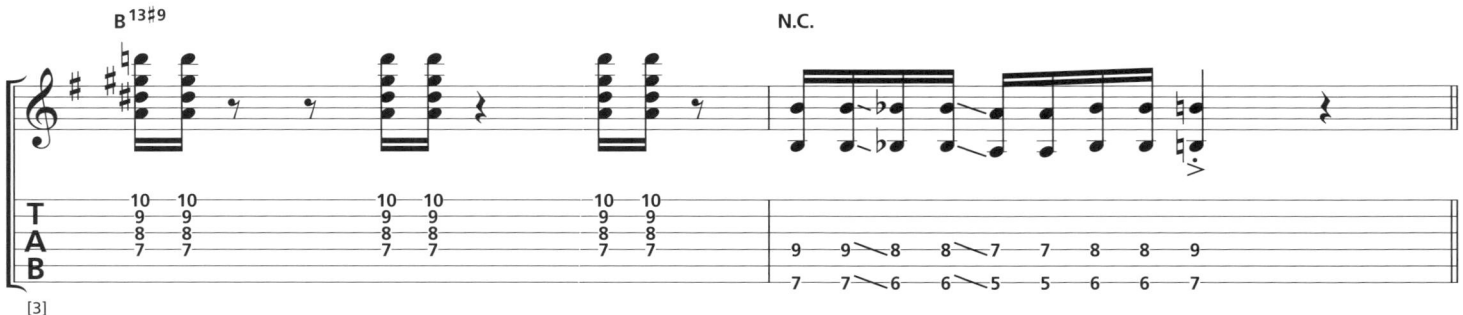
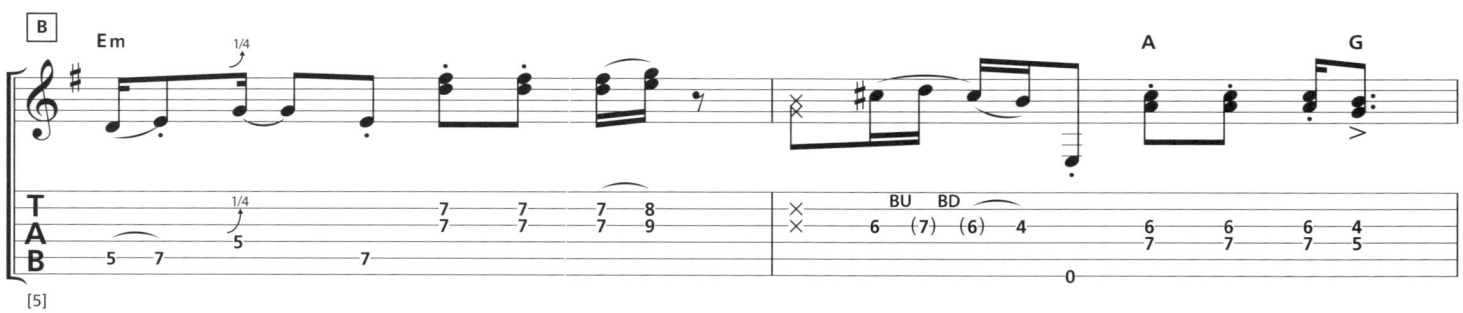
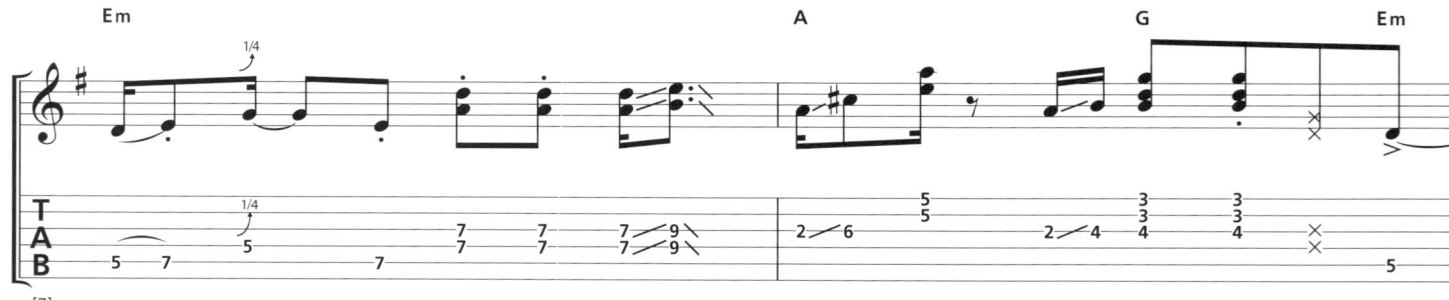

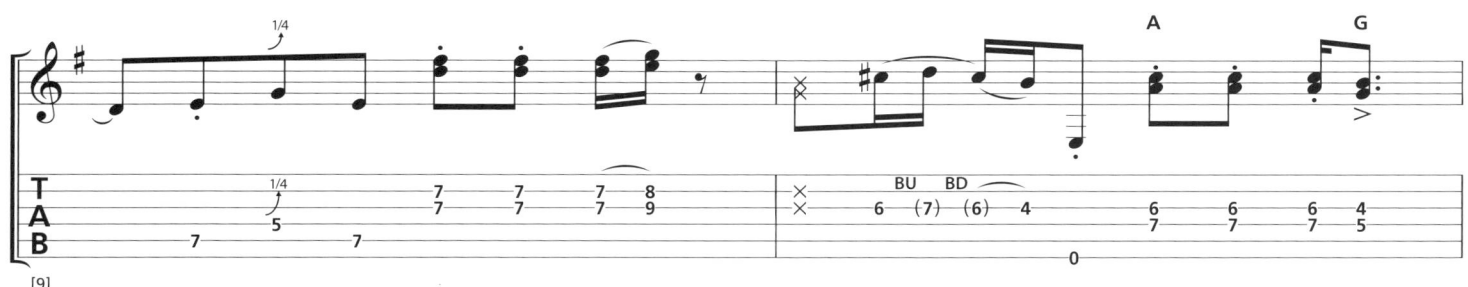
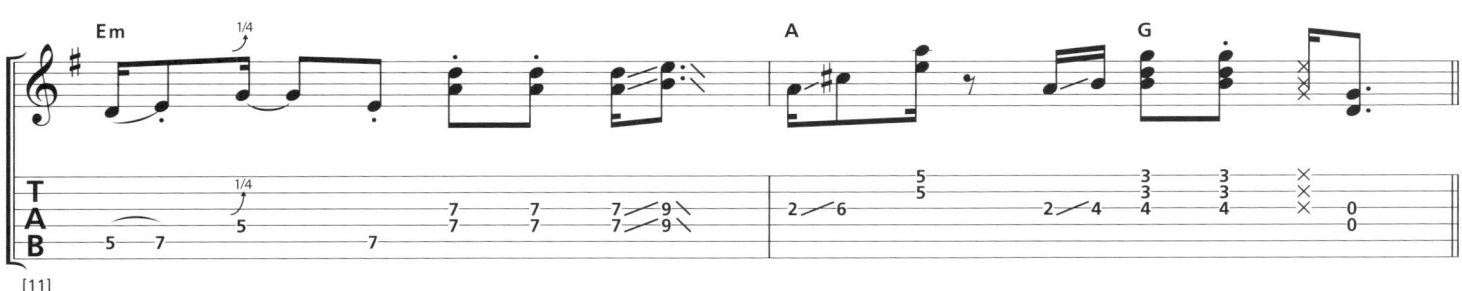
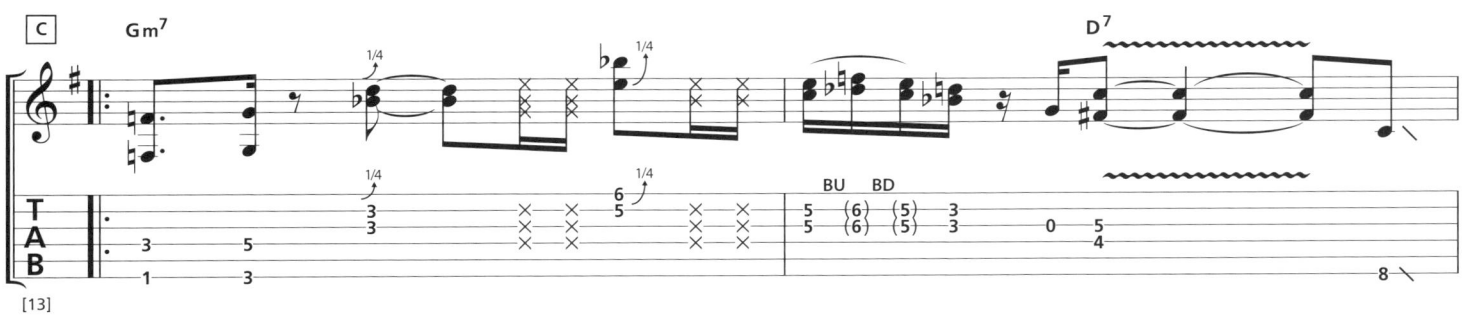

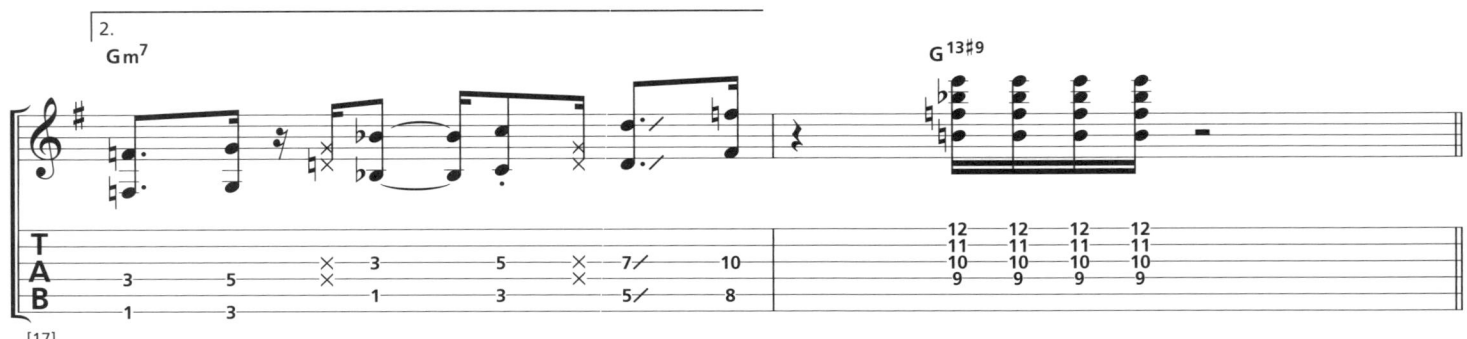

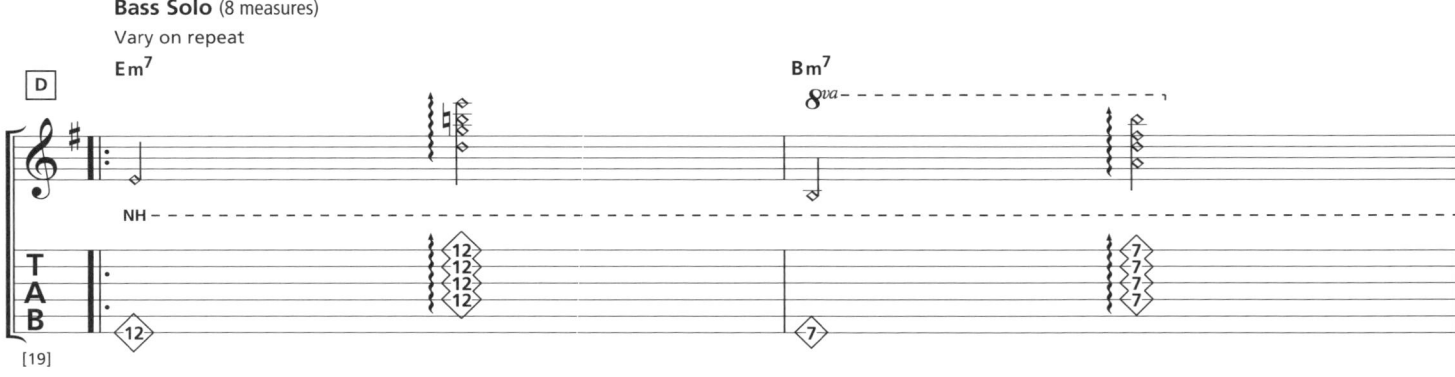

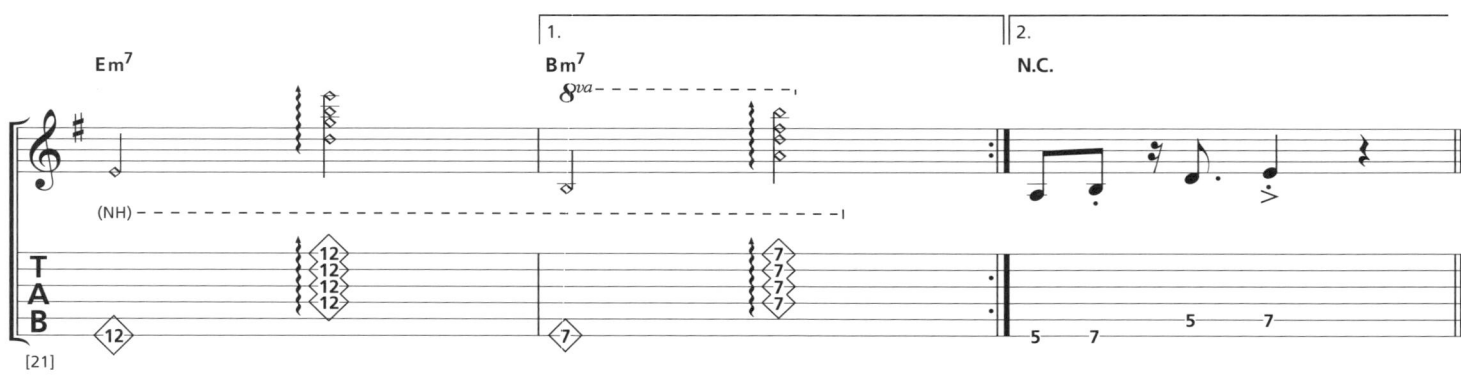

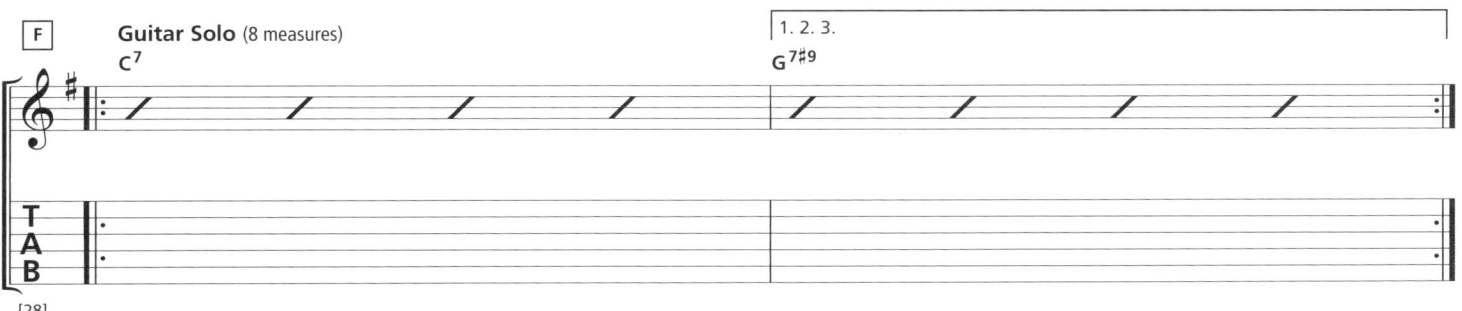
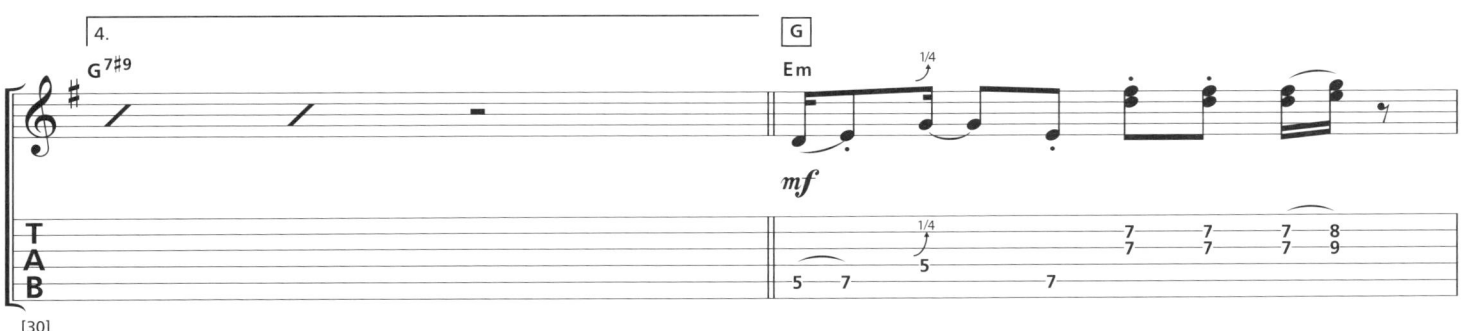

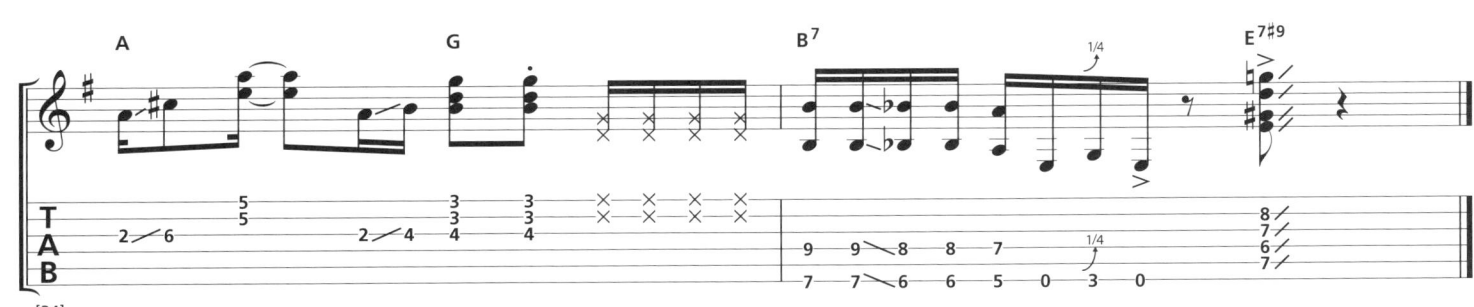

Walkthrough

Amp Settings
Aim for a well rounded clean tone with some reverb and a distorted tone with a heavy overdrive (with the gain set to around 7 or 8). If you are using an effects pedal for both sounds, check that the balance is correct between the two individual tones.

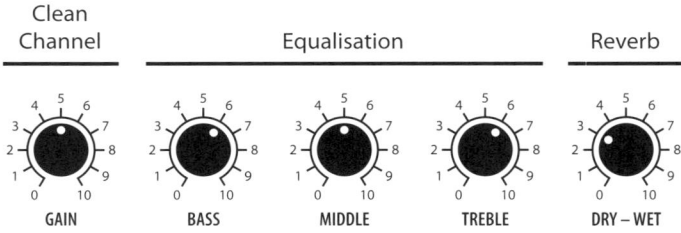

A Section (Measures 1–4)
The A section is a syncopated chordal part that ends with a low-string octave run.

Measures 1–3 | *Complex chord names*
While the opening $B^{13\sharp 9}$ chord may look somewhat intimidating, closer inspection reveals that this complex name is the literal spelling of a simple fretboard shape that is easier to play than the notation suggests.

B Section (Measures 5–12)
The section is a funky riff that utilises a range of articulations and techniques to vary the basic pattern.

Measure 5 | *Double-stop hammer-on*
Here you will need to play the 7th fret notes with your first finger and hammer-on with your second and third fingers, applying equal force with both fingers so that the two notes are balanced (Fig. 2).

C Section (Measures 13–18)
The C section combines low octaves with high double-stops and single notes.

Measure 14 | *Double-stop bend*
This double-stop bend should be played with your third finger on both frets supported by your first and second fingers to add strength and control. As you push or pull the string, maintain pressure *into* the fretboard to keep the note ringing for the duration of the bend.

D Section (Measures 19–23)
The D section is the bass solo where the guitar plays a part built entirely on natural harmonics. The repeat gives you an opportunity to vary the part.

Measures 19–22 | *Natural harmonics*
Your finger placement for the 7th fret harmonics must be precise so don't be discouraged if it takes a while to sound them correctly.

E Section (Measures 24–27)
The E section takes full advantage of the slow tempo to create a heavy groove.

Measures 24–27 | *Tight rhythm playing*
At slow tempos it is easy to rush long notes like those found in measures 24–27. Practise with a metronome, concentrating on playing the first note of each beat exactly at the same time as the metronome click.

F & G Sections (Measures 28–35)
The F section is the guitar solo; the G section a reprise of B.

Measure 28–30 | *Guitar solo*
Although the first chord of the guitar solo is C^7, the solo is in the key of G. The G minor pentatonic or blues scales are the most obvious choices.

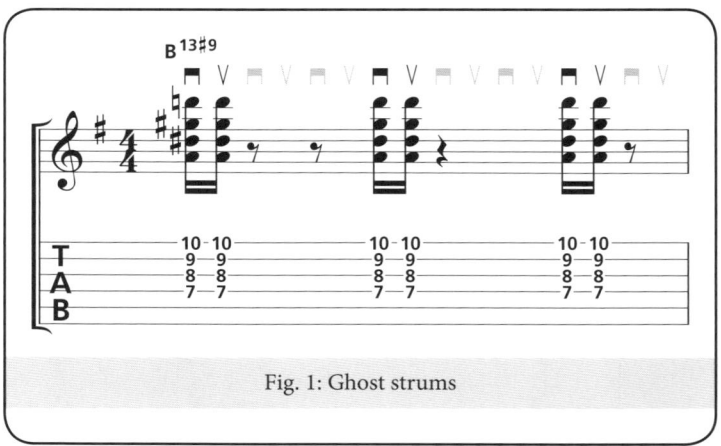

Fig. 1: Ghost strums

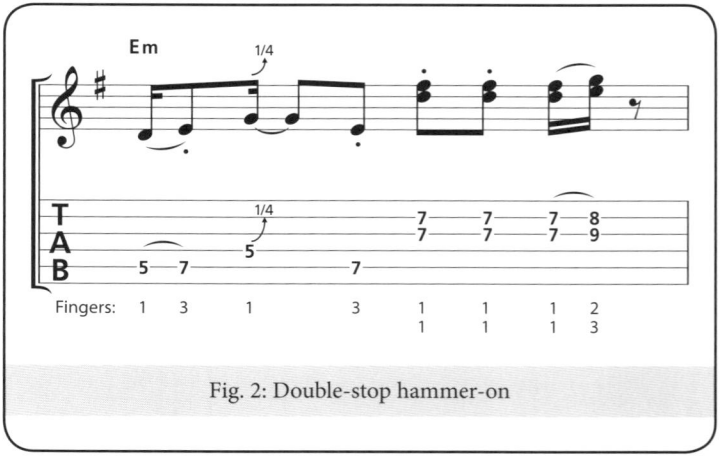

Fig. 2: Double-stop hammer-on

Technical Exercises

In this section the assessor will ask you to play a selection of exercises drawn from each of the four groups shown below. Groups A, B and C contain examples of the scales, arpeggios and chords you can use when playing the pieces. In Group D you will be asked to prepare the riff exercise and play it to the backing track in the assessment. You do not need to memorise the exercises (and can use the book in the assessment) but the assessor will be looking for the speed of your response. The assessor will also give credit for the level of your musicality.

Before you start the section you will be asked whether you would like to play the exercises along with the click or hear a single measure of click before you commence the test. The tempo is ♩ = 80.

Groups A and B should be prepared in two octaves in two positions. The first position is to be prepared on the E string from the starting notes of F, G and A. The second position is to be prepared on the A string from the starting notes of B, C and D. You may have to make adjustments for open strings in your fingerings of some scales. For each position, the assessor will choose from a starting note of either F, G, A (E string) or B, C, D (A string).

Below is a full list of *everything* you need to prepare for the Technical Exercises section of the assessment. The examples on the following pages are a *sample* of what you need to need to prepare. The fingerings shown are suggestions and you may use any alternative you like provided the scale or arpeggio starts from the string specified. A full set of fingering suggestions in all the keys listed below is available in the *Rockschool Guitar Technical Handbook*.

Technical Summary

Tempo	♩ = 80
Scales | Major	F, G & A (on the E string) B, C & D (on the A string)
Scales | Natural Minor	F, G & A (on the E string) B, C & D (on the A string)
Scales | Harmonic Minor	F, G & A (on the E string) B, C & D (on the A string)
Scales | Minor Pentatonic	F, G & A (on the E string) B, C & D (on the A string)
Scales | Major Pentatonic	F, G & A (on the E string) B, C & D (on the A string)
Scales | Blues	F, G & A (on the E string) B, C & D (on the A string)
Arpeggios | Major	F, G & A (on the E string) B, C & D (on the A string)
Arpeggios | Minor	F, G & A (on the E string) B, C & D (on the A string)
Chords | Triads	Major & Minor (three inversions) Sequence in C
Riff	Eight measures @ ♩ = 100

Technical Exercises

Group A: Scales

1. Major scale (F major shown, root on E string)

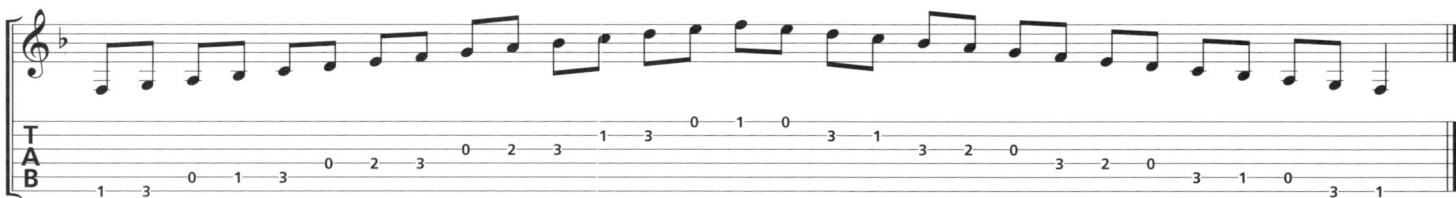

2. Natural minor scale (B natural minor shown, root on A string)

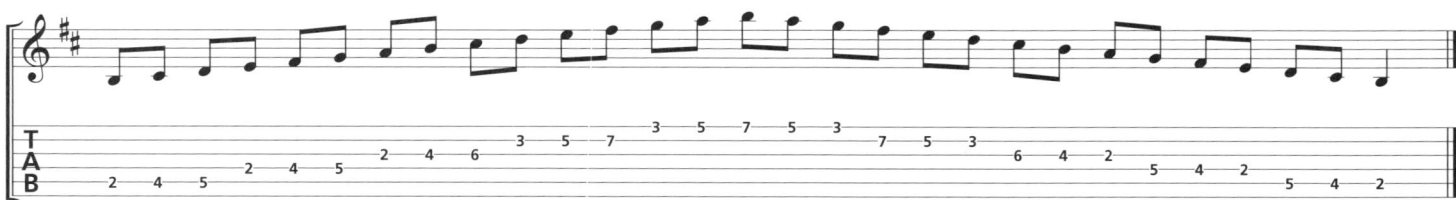

3. Harmonic minor scale (A harmonic minor shown, root on E string)

4. Minor pentatonic scale (G minor pentatonic shown, root on E string)

5. Major pentatonic (D major pentatonic shown, root on A string)

6. Blues scale (C blues scale shown, root on A string)

Technical Exercises

Group B: Arpeggios

1. Major arpeggio (G major arpeggio shown, root on E string)

2. Minor arpeggio (C minor arpeggio shown, root on A string)

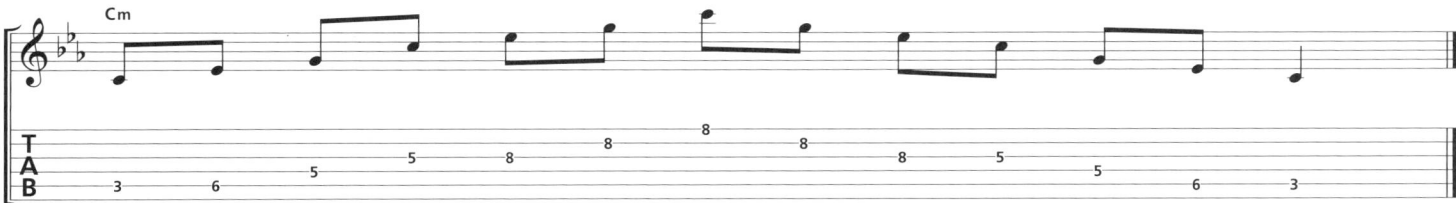

Group C: Chords

Major and minor triads played in three inversions on the top three strings in the key of C. To be played in a continuous sequence.

1. Major and minor triads in three inversions

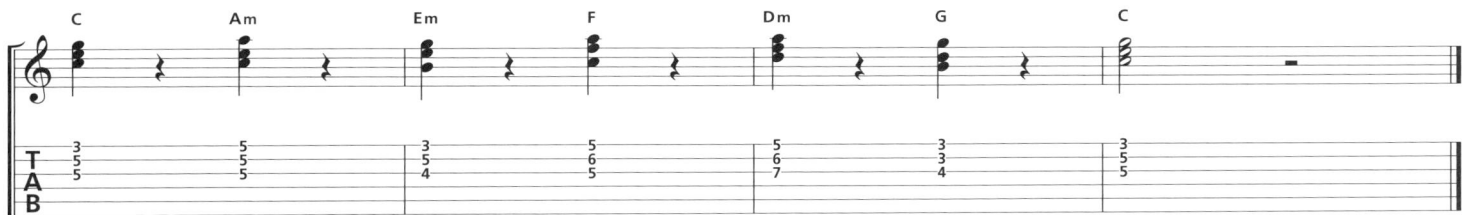

Group D: Riff

In the assessment you will be asked to play the following riff to a backing track. The riff shown in measures 1 and 2 should be played in the same shape in measures 3–8. The root note of the pattern to be played is shown in the music in measures 3, 5 and 7. The tempo is ♩ = 100.

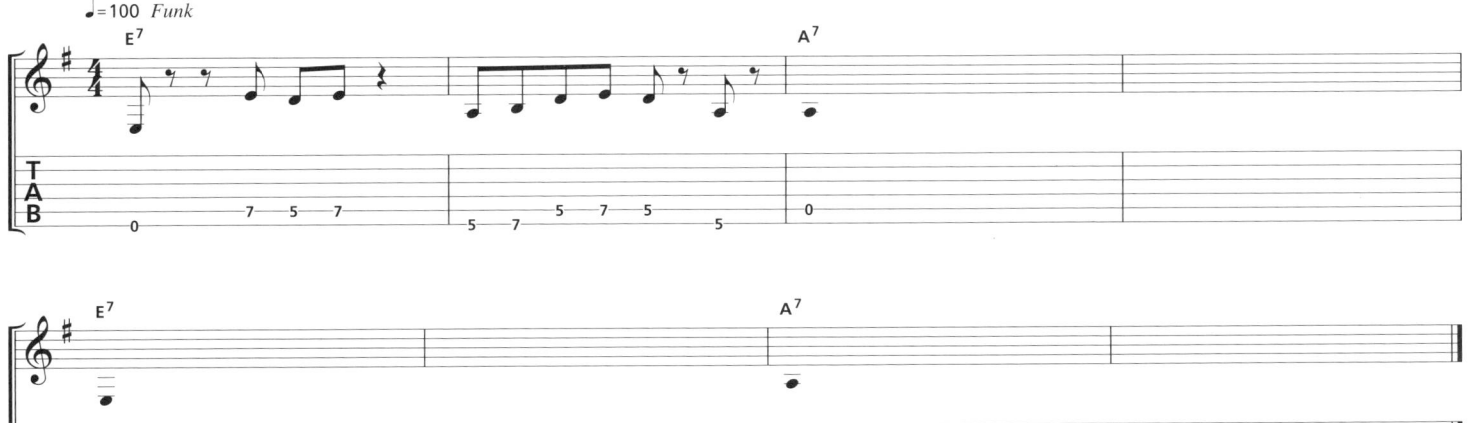

Sight Reading

In this section you have a choice between either a Sight Reading test or an Improvisation & Interpretation test (see facing page). At this level there is an element of improvisation. This is in the form of a two measure ending. The piece will be composed in the style of rock, funk or blues and will have chord symbols throughout. The test is eight measures long and is in one of the four following keys: F major or G major, or E minor or G minor.

The improvised ending will use chord patterns that have been used in the sight reading part of the test. The assessor will allow you 90 seconds to prepare it and will set the tempo for you. The tempo is ♩=90.

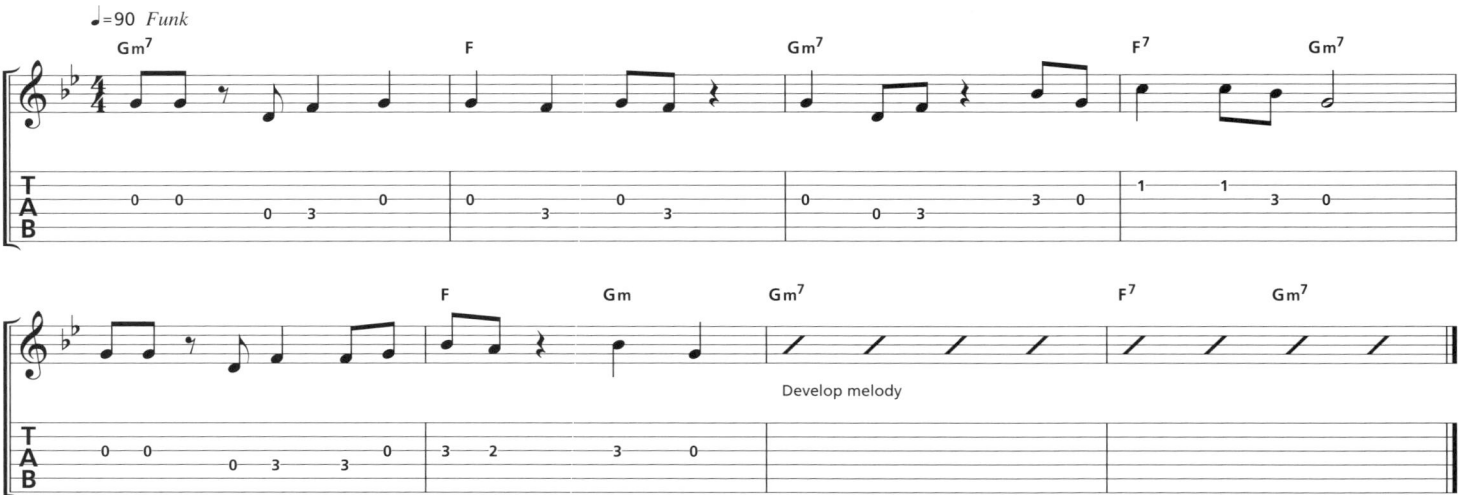

Improvisation & Interpretation

In Level/Grade 5, the Improvisation & Interpretation test contains a small amount of sight reading. This consists of a two measure section of rhythm notation at the beginning of the test. You will be asked to play the chords in the rhythms indicated and complete the test using an improvised line made up of chords and lead lines where indicated. This is played to a backing track of no more than eight measures. The test will be given in one of the four following keys: A major or G major, or E minor or G minor. You have 30 seconds to prepare and then you will be allowed to practise during the first playing of the backing track before playing it to the assessor on the second playing of the backing track. This test is continuous with a one measure count-in at the beginning and after the practice session. The tempo is ♩=90–100.

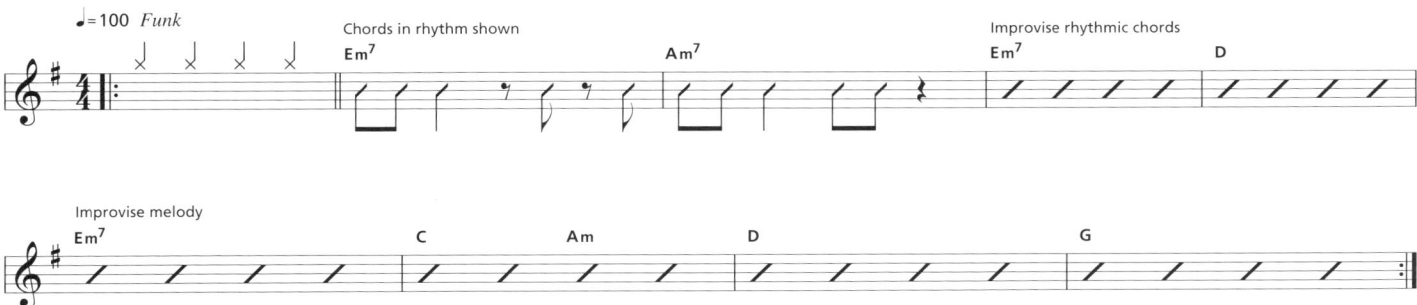

Ear Tests

There are two Ear Tests in this level/grade. The assessor will play each test to you twice. You will find one example of each type of test printed below.

Test 1: Melodic Recall
The assessor will play you a two-measure melody with a drum backing using either the D major pentatonic or A minor pentatonic scales. The first note of the melody will be the root note and the first interval will be descending. You will play the melody back on your instrument. You will hear the test twice.

Each time the test is played the sequence is: count-in, root note, count-in, melody. There will be a short gap for you to practise after you have heard the test for the second time. You will hear the count-in and root note for the third time followed by a *vocal* count-in and you will then play the melody to the drum backing. The tempo is ♩=90.

Test 2: Harmonic Recall
The assessor will play you a tonic chord followed by a four-measure chord sequence in the key of G major played to a drum backing. The sequence will be drawn from the I, IV, V and vi chords and may occur in any combination. You will be asked to play the chord sequence to the drum backing in the rhythm shown in the example below. This rhythm will be used in all examples of this test given in the assessment. You will then be asked to identify the sequence you have played to the assessor. You will hear the test twice.

Each time the test is played the sequence is: count-in, tonic, count-in, chords. There will be a short gap for you to practise after you have heard the test for the second time. You will hear the count-in and tonic for the third time followed by a *vocal* count-in then you will play the chords to the drum backing. You should then name the chord sequence, including chord types (i.e. major or minor). The tempo is ♩=80.

General Musicianship Questions

In this part of the assessment you will be asked five questions. Four of these questions will be about general music knowledge and the fifth question asked will be about your instrument.

Music Knowledge
The assessor will ask you the four music knowledge questions based on a piece of music that you have played in the assessment. You will nominate the piece of music about which the questions will be asked. The scale question at the end of the list of subjects is mandatory.

In Level/Grade 5 you will be asked to identify/explain:

- The names of pitches

- The meaning of accidentals: ♯ (sharp), ♭ (flat) and ♮ (natural) signs

- The meaning of the time signature, key signature and swing time markings

- Repeat marks, first and second time measures, *D.C.*, *D.S.*, *al Coda* and *al Fine* markings

- Hammer-ons, pull-offs, accents and vibrato markings

- The construction of minor ^{7}, major ^{7} or dominant ^{7} chords

- One type of scale that can be used appropriately in the solo section of the piece you have played

Instrument Knowledge
The assessor will also ask you one question regarding your instrument.

In Level/Grade 5 you will be asked to identify/explain:

- Any part or control on your guitar

- The function of the volume and tone controls on your guitar

- The tone settings for the piece you have played on the amp and why you have chosen these settings

Further Information
Tips on how to approach this part of this assessment can be found in the *Syllabus Guide* for guitar, the Rockschool *Guitar Companion Guide* and on the Rockschool website: *www.rslawards.com*. The Introduction to Tone, a comprehensive explanation of guitar tones, can be found at the back of each level/grade book and the tone guide to each piece is in the appropriate Walkthrough.

Marking Schemes

DEBUT TO LEVEL/GRADE 5 *

ELEMENT	PASS	MERIT	DISTINCTION
Performance Piece 1	12–14 out of 20	15–17 out of 20	18+ out of 20
Performance Piece 2	12–14 out of 20	15–17 out of 20	18+ out of 20
Performance Piece 3	12–14 out of 20	15–17 out of 20	18+ out of 20
Technical Exercises	9–10 out of 15	11–12 out of 15	13+ out of 15
Sight Reading *or* Improvisation & Interpretation	6 out of 10	7–8 out of 10	9+ out of 10
Ear Tests	6 out of 10	7–8 out of 10	9+ out of 10
General Musicianship Questions	3 out of 5	4 out of 5	5 out of 5
TOTAL MARKS	60%+	74%+	90%+

LEVELS/GRADES 6–8

ELEMENT	PASS	MERIT	DISTINCTION
Performance Piece 1	12–14 out of 20	15–17 out of 20	18+ out of 20
Performance Piece 2	12–14 out of 20	15–17 out of 20	18+ out of 20
Performance Piece 3	12–14 out of 20	15–17 out of 20	18+ out of 20
Technical Exercises	9–10 out of 15	11–12 out of 15	13+ out of 15
Quick Study Piece	6 out of 10	7–8 out of 10	9+ out of 10
Ear Tests	6 out of 10	7–8 out of 10	9+ out of 10
General Musicianship Questions	3 out of 5	4 out of 5	5 out of 5
TOTAL MARKS	60%+	74%+	90%+

PERFORMANCE CERTIFICATES | DEBUT TO LEVEL/GRADE 8 *

ELEMENT	PASS	MERIT	DISTINCTION
Performance Piece 1	12–14 out of 20	15–17 out of 20	18+ out of 20
Performance Piece 2	12–14 out of 20	15–17 out of 20	18+ out of 20
Performance Piece 3	12–14 out of 20	15–17 out of 20	18+ out of 20
Performance Piece 4	12–14 out of 20	15–17 out of 20	18+ out of 20
Performance Piece 5	12–14 out of 20	15–17 out of 20	18+ out of 20
TOTAL MARKS	60%+	75%+	90%+

* Note that there are no Debut Vocal assessments.

Entering Rockschool Assessments

Entering a Rockschool assessment is easy, just go online and follow our simple six step process. All details for entering online, dates, fees, regulations and Free Choice pieces can be found at *www.rslawards.com*

- All candidates should ensure they bring their own Level/Grade syllabus book to the assessment or have proof of digital purchase ready to show the assessor.

- All Level/Grade 6–8 candidates must ensure that they bring valid photo ID to their assessment.

Mechanical Copyright Information

Lose Yourself
(Mathers/Bass/Resto)
Kobalt Music Publishing Limited

Love On Top
(Nash/Knowles/Taylor)
EMI Music Publishing Limited/Warner/Chappell North America Limited/Downtown Music UK Limited

People Say
(Neville/Nocentelli/Porter/Modeliste)
BMG Rights Management (UK) Limited

Pick Up The Pieces
(Ball/Gorrie/Duncan/McIntosh/McIntyre/Stuart)
Fairwood Music Limited/BMG Rights Management (UK) Limited/Wixen Music UK Limited

Lay Down Sally
(Clapton/Terry/Levy)
Throat Music Limited

Hell Ain't A Bad Place To Be
(Young/Young/Scott)
BMG Rights Management (UK) Limited

mcps

Introduction to Tone

A large part of an effective guitar performance is selecting the right tone. The electric guitar's sound is subject to a wide range of variables, and this guide outlines the basic controls present on most amplifiers as well as the common variations between models. There is also a basic overview of pickups and the effect their location on the guitar has on tone. Finally, it covers the differences between the types of distortion, which is crucial to getting your basic sound right.

At Level/Grade 5 the tone may change within the course of a piece. You should aim to use a tone that is stylistically appropriate and you may bring your own equipment to the assessment room for this purpose. There is a tone guide at the start of each Walkthrough to help you.

Basic amplifier controls

Most amplifiers come with a standard set of controls that are the same as, or very similar to, the diagram below. It's important to understand what each control is and the effect that it has on your guitar's tone.

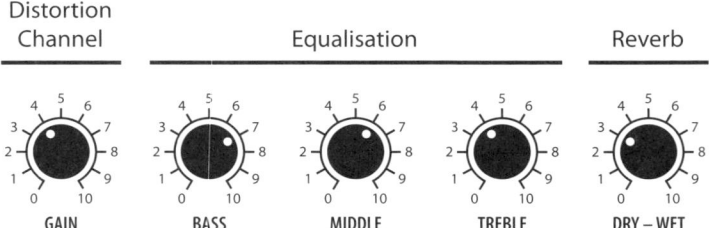

- **Channel (Clean/Distortion)**
  Most amplifiers have two channels that can be selected either by a switch on the amp or a footswitch. One channel is usually 'clean' while the other can be driven harder to create a distorted (or 'dirty') tone. If your amp doesn't have two channels, look at the 'variation of basic controls' below to see how to get clean and dirty tones from a one channel amp.

  - **Gain**
    In simple terms, the gain determines how hard you drive the amp. This governs how distorted the dirty (also called 'drive', 'overdrive', or 'distortion') channel is and acts as a second volume control on the clean channel (though a high gain setting will distort even the clean channel).

  - **Bass**
    This adjusts the lowest frequencies. Boost it to add warmth and reduce or 'cut' it if your sound is muddy or woolly.

  - **Middle**
    This is the most important equalisation (often shortened to just 'EQ') control. Most of the guitar's tonal character is found in the mid-range so adjusting this control has a lot of impact upon your tone. Boosting it with a dirty sound will create a more classic rock tone while cutting it will produce a more metal one.

  - **Treble**
    This adjusts the high frequencies. Boost it to add brightness and cut it if the sound is too harsh or brittle.

  - **Reverb**
    Short for 'reverberation'. This artificially recreates the ambience of your guitar in a large room, usually a hall. This dial controls the balance between the 'dry' (the sound without the reverb) and 'wet' (the sound with the reverb) sounds.

Variations of basic controls

The diagram above shows the most common amp controls. There are many variations to this basic setup, which can often be confusing. The following section is a breakdown of some of the other amp controls you may encounter:

- **Presence control**
  Sometimes this dial replaces the 'middle' control and other times it appears in addition to it. It adjusts the higher mid-range frequencies (those found between the 'middle' and 'treble' dials).

- **No reverb control**
  Reverb can be a nice addition to your guitar tone but it's not essential. Don't be concerned if your amp doesn't have a reverb control.

- **Volume, gain, master setup**
  Single channel amplifiers often have an extra volume control (in addition to the master volume) located next to the gain control. For clean sounds, keep the gain set low and the volume similarly low and use the master control for overall volume. If the master control is on 10 and you require more level, turn the volume control up. However, you may find that this starts to distort as you reach the higher numbers.

  To get a distorted tone, turn the volume down low and the gain up until you get the amount of distortion you require. Regulate the overall level with master volume. If the master control is on 10 and you require more level simply turn the volume up. In this case, however, you may find you lose clarity before you reach maximum.

Pickups

Entire books have been devoted to the intricacies of pickups. However, three basic pieces of information will help you understand a lot about your guitar tone:

- **Singlecoils**
  These narrow pickups are fitted to many guitars. The Fender Stratocaster is the most famous guitar fitted with singlecoils. They produce a bright, cutting sound that can sound a little thin in some situations, especially heavier styles of rock music.

- **Humbuckers**
  This type of pickup was originally designed to remove or 'buck' the hum produced by singlecoil pickups, hence the name. They produce a warm, mellow sound compared to singlecoil pickups but have a tendency to sound a little muddy in some situations. They are usually identifiable because they are twice the width of a singlecoil pickup. The Gibson Les Paul is a well-known guitar fitted with humbucking pickups.

- **Pickup location**
  Basically, pickups located near the guitar's neck will have the warmest sound and those located near the bridge will have the brightest sound.

Different types of 'dirty' tones

There are lots of different words to describe the 'dirty' guitar sounds. In fact, all the sounds are 'distortions' of the clean tone, which can be confusing when you consider there's a 'type' of distortion called 'distortion'. Below is a simplified breakdown of the three main types of dirty sounds, plus some listening material to help you through this tonal minefield:

- **Overdrive**
  This is the 'mildest' form of distortion. It can be quite subtle and only evident when the guitar is played strongly. It can also be full-on and aggressive.
  Hear it on: Cream – 'Sunshine Of Your Love', AC/DC – 'Back In Black', Oasis – 'Cigarettes and Alcohol'.

- **Distortion**
  This is usually associated with heavier styles of music. It's dense and the most extreme of the dirty tones and is usually associated with heavy styles of music.
  Hear it on: Metallica – 'Enter Sandman', Avenged Sevenfold – 'Bat Country', Bon Jovi – 'You Give Love A Bad Name'.

- **Fuzz**
  As the name implies, fuzz is a broken, 'fuzzy' sound. It was popular in the 1960s but, while still evident in certain genres, it's less common now.
  Hear it on: Jimi Hendrix Experience – 'Purple Haze', The Kinks – 'You Really Got Me'.

Guitar Notation Explained

THE MUSICAL STAVE shows pitches and rhythms and is divided by lines into measures. Pitches are named after the first seven letters of the alphabet.

TABLATURE graphically represents the guitar fingerboard. Each horizontal line represents a string and each number represents a fret.

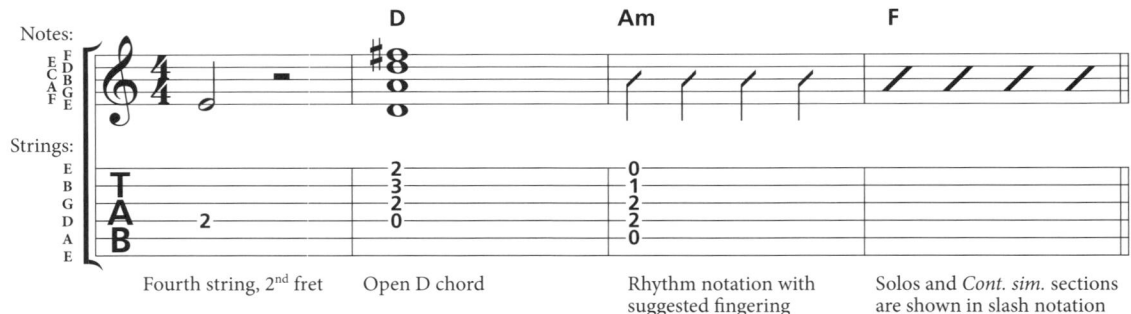

Fourth string, 2nd fret   Open D chord   Rhythm notation with suggested fingering   Solos and *Cont. sim.* sections are shown in slash notation

Definitions For Special Guitar Notation

HAMMER-ON: Pick the lower note, then sound the higher note by fretting it without picking.

PULL-OFF: Pick the higher note then sound the lower note by lifting the finger without picking.

SLIDE: Pick the first note and slide to the next. If the line connects (as below) the second note is *not* repicked.

GLISSANDO: Slide off of a note at the end of its rhythmic value. The note that follows *is* repicked.

STRING BENDS: Pick the first note then bend (or release the bend) to the pitch indicated in brackets.

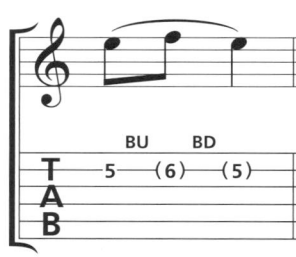

VIBRATO: Vibrate the note by bending and releasing the string smoothly and continuously.

TRILL: Rapidly alternate between the two bracketed notes by hammering on and pulling off.

NATURAL HARMONICS: Lightly touch the string above the indicated fret then pick to sound a harmonic.

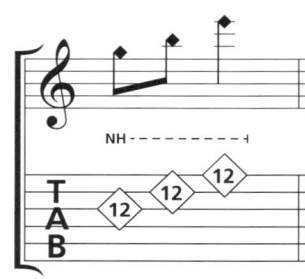

PINCHED HARMONICS: Bring the thumb of the picking hand into contact with the string immediately after the pick.

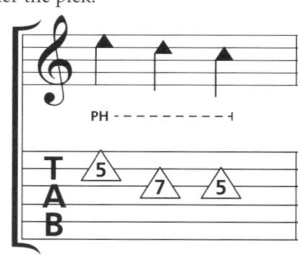

PICK-HAND TAP: Strike the indicated note with a finger from the picking hand. Usually followed by a pull-off.

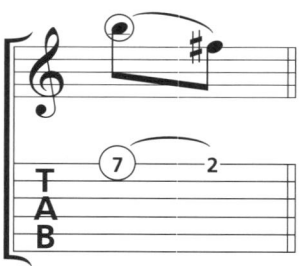

FRET-HAND TAP: As pick-hand tap, but use fretting hand. Usually followed by a pull-off or hammer-on.

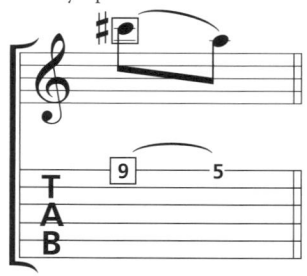

QUARTER-TONE BEND: Pick the note indicated and bend the string up by a quarter tone.

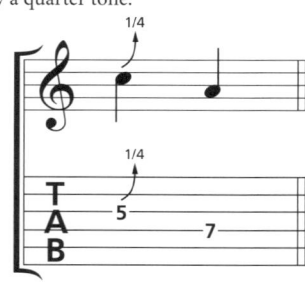

PRE-BENDS: Before picking the note, bend the string from the fret indicated between the staves, to the equivalent pitch indicated in brackets in the TAB.

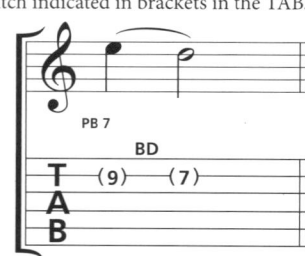

WHAMMY BAR BEND: Use the whammy bar to bend notes to the pitches indicated in brackets in the TAB.

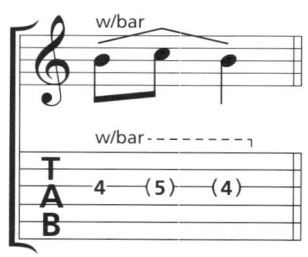

D.%. al Coda

D.C. al Fine

- Go back to the sign (%), then play until the measure marked **To Coda** ⊕ then skip to the section marked ⊕ **Coda**.

- Go back to the beginning of the song and play until the measure marked **Fine** (end).

- Repeat the measures between the repeat signs.

- When a repeated section has different endings, play the first ending only the first time and the second ending only the second time.